GEARED FOR GREATNESS
100 THINGS I TAUGHT MY CHILDREN

Fourth Edition

Yvonne D. Camper

GEARED FOR GREATNESS

© 2016 Yvonne D. Camper

Published by Quiver Full Publishing
7426 Cherry Street Suite 210-310, Fontana, CA 92336

First Edition Published in 2008

Printed in the United States of America

All rights reserved. No part of this publication may be reproduced, stored in a retrieval system, or transmitted in any form or by any means-for example, electronic, photocopy, recording-without the prior written permission of the publisher. The only exception is brief quotations in printed review. Every effort has been made to determine and acknowledge copyrights, but in some cases copyright could not be traced. The author offers apologies for any such omission and will rectify this in subsequent editions upon notification to the following email address: yvonnedcamper@gmail.com

New King James Version® (NKJV). Copyright © 1982 by Thomas Nelson. Used by permission. All rights reserved.

New American Standard Bible ® La Habra, CA: Foundation Publications, for the Lockman Foundation, 1971. Used by permission. All rights reserved.

The Contemporary English Version Copyright ® 1995 American Bible Society. Used by permission. All rights reserved.

The Holy Bible, King James Version. Cambridge Edition: 1769; King James Bible Online, 2017. www.kingjamesbibleonline.org.

ISBN-13: 978-0-9988391-4-1
ISBN-10: 0998839140

100 Things I Taught My Children

Dedication

This book is dedicated to and written for my children. I am grateful that God chose such amazing people for me to fashion, nurture, and release into the world. Brianne Elizabeth, Roman Lee IV, Aubrie Zion, Christian Judah, and Benjamin Matthew. I am honored to be your mother.

To my grandchildren Journi and Judah and two more on the way, I am honored to be your Grammy. May you carry on the legacy that this family is building. To my husband, Vince, thank you for your love, friendship and support.

To all my nieces and nephews, you are outstanding individuals, and I am very proud to be part of your journey. And to Robin, Anthony, Angela, and Christopher, I am so thankful that God blessed me with such wonderful siblings.

To my mother, Gwendolyn Elizabeth Dozier (December 1949 - June 1982), life without you has been hard. I can't believe it has already been 32 years since you have been gone but the older I get, the more I am grateful that God chose you. There are so many lessons you taught us that have enriched my life and the life of those that I touch. Your legacy lives on. To my father, James Sebastian, you are a brilliant and gifted man. I am proud and grateful to be your daughter.

To my maternal grandparents, Francis and Martha Dozier, what an awesome privilege it was to be able to spend life learning from you. You both were a constant source of support and encouragement. You will forever live on in my spirit.

CONTENTS

Acknowledgements .... *xi*

Forward .... *xiii*

Preface .... *xv*

Chance or Purpose? .... - 1 -

Incredible Gift .... - 3 -

Be the First to Say Hello .... - 4 -

Don't Break Rank .... - 5 -

The Lost Art of Marriage .... - 6 -

Affirmation #1 .... - 8 -

Lead, Don't Follow .... - 10 -

Never Too Busy to Listen .... - 11 -

Hugs and Kisses Last a Lifetime .... - 13 -

Heart of Compassion .... - 14 -

Parenting Is Seasonal .... - 15 -

Be Responsible .... - 16 -

Affirmation #2 .... - 17 -

The Big Brute .... - 19 -

Be A Valuable Employee .... - 20 -

Focus - The Key to Success .... - 21 -

The Power of Self-Control .... - 22 -

Mind Your Manners .... - 23 -

Affirmation #3 .... - 24 -

Speak Up! .... - 26 -

The Rewards of Discipline .... - 28 -

The Power of Family and Friends .... - 30 -

My, How Time Flies .... - 32 -

The Value of Loyalty .... - 33 -

Affirmation #4 .... - 34 -

Don't Compromise Who You Are .... - 36 -

Never Say Can't .... - 37 -

In His Image .... - 39 -

Soar with Eagles .... - 40 -

Dare to Be Great .... - 41 -

Munificent Giving .... - 44 -

Encourage Creativity .... - 45 -

Wisdom Is the Principal Thing .... - 46 -

The Power of Forgiveness .... - 47 -

100 Things I Taught My Children

GEARED FOR GREATNESS

Affirmation #6	- 49 -
The Gift of Closure	- 52 -
Two Are Better Than One	- 53 -
Count Your Blessings	- 54 -
Pay Attention to Details	- 55 -
Don't Over-Stimulate Your Child	- 56 -
Failure and Adversity	- 59 -
Certificate of Authenticity	- 62 -
The Power of Integrity	- 63 -
Equity	- 64 -
The Power of The Tongue	- 65 -
Attitude	- 68 -
Be Self-Motivated	- 69 -
Boundaries Are Important	- 70 -
No Job Is Beneath You	- 71 -
Clean Up After Yourself	- 72 -
Affirmation #9	- 73 -
You Are Valuable	- 75 -
Reaping and Sowing	- 76 -

GEARED FOR GREATNESS

Choose Your Battles Wisely .... - 77 -

The Gift of Laughter .... - 78 -

One Person Can Change the World .... - 79 -

Read! Read! Read! .... - 82 -

First Impressions .... - 84 -

Say Cheese! .... - 85 -

Be an Optimist .... - 86 -

If at First You Don't Succeed… .... - 89 -

Choose Your Mentors Wisely .... - 90 -

Opportunities Are Created .... - 91 -

Divine Contentment .... - 92 -

Don't Fear Death .... - 93 -

Affirmation #12 .... - 95 -

Don't Worry .... - 97 -

Only What You Do for Christ Will Last .... - 98 -

Be Prepared .... - 99 -

Make Wise Choices .... - 100 -

Be Resilient .... - 101 -

Don't Abuse Your Authority .... - 104 -

Practice What You Preach	- 105 -
Love Never Fails	- 106 -
You Cannot Fail If You Do Your Best	- 107 -
Work Hard	- 108 -
Affirmation #14	- 109 -
Know When to Help	- 111 -
Apology Accepted	- 112 -
Replaceable You	- 113 -
Don't Take Shortcuts	- 115 -
Don't Measure Success by Possessions	- 116 -
Fearless!	- 117 -
Respect Nature	- 118 -
Obedience, The Ultimate Quality	- 123 -
The Green-Eyed Monster	- 124 -
The Dangers of Greed	- 127 -
Wealth or Prosperity?	- 128 -
Pride, Arrogance, And Confidence - The Distinction	- 131 -
Keep Your Word	- 133 -
The Golden Rule	- 134 -

GEARED FOR GREATNESS

Choose Joy - 135 -

Drinking, Driving and Drugs .... - 136 -

Affirmation #17 .... - 137 -

To Know Thyself .... - 141 -

Guard Your Heart .... - 142 -

Dreams Do Come True .... - 143 -

Manage Your Health .... - 144 -

Stay Educated .... - 146 -

Affirmation #18 .... - 147 -

Patience Is a Virtue .... - 150 -

Money and Credit Smarts .... - 151 -

Finish Strong .... - 153 -

The Power of Prayer .... - 154 -

Rejection and Criticism .... - 155 -

Lessons in Dating .... - 156 -

Social Media and Texting: Blessing or Curse? .... - 157 -

Affirmation #19 .... - 160 -

Your Child's 30-day Emotional Makeover .... - 163 -

Final Thoughts .... - 194 -

Acknowledgements

Last and certainly not least, I want to thank Rae Lockett, Kathy Levinson and Phyllis Siteman for their contribution in making this book a reality. I also want to dedicate this book to my dear friend Petra Gonzales who went home to be with the Lord in 2015. Her contributions to this book were valuable and priceless. Rest well my friend, you are certainly missed.

Forward

During my childhood, my mom gave me many gems of wisdom and instruction that I did not heed because I thought that firsthand experience would be the best teacher and that I knew best. Now, at the age of 32 and during raising my own children, I realize that listening to my mother would have saved me many years of unnecessary struggles. I now have a firm understanding that God has a strategic plan for every person's life, and He places parents as instructors to help us navigate the difficult terrains. Parents, don't give up.

    I am sure parents will endure many sleepless nights wondering if their children are embracing the wisdom and instruction that is being shared with them. Although it might seem like they aren't listening, embrace the fact that none of your words will wither away. You are simply the farmer planting the seeds and tending to the land to ensure that you will reap an abundant harvest. Remember that the law of the land still applies: what you sow, you will also reap. Therefore, sow a good seed, and you will reap a good harvest. Unfortunately, God didn't promise the harvest would be an instantaneous one! Stay faithful in your parenting.

    Finally, children, don't give into the lies that parents don't know what they are talking about or parents just don't understand. God has placed our parents as our help for a reason; we must accept, honor, and follow with diligence the words they speak into our lives. We might not always agree, but the Bible teaches that "obedience is better than sacrifice" and urges children to obey their parents so their "days may be long." God gives tremendous rewards to those who heed the wisdom and instruction given to them and walk in the path of obedience. It is my hope that while you read this book, you will be enlightened and inspired. That you will grow as a parent, and your wisdom will become even greater.

    Mom, even though I probably didn't listen to all the hundreds of things you taught me while I was growing up, please be assured that your labor was not in vain; it has brought forth much fruit. Each day, I grow stronger because I can pull from the wisdom you instilled in me to overcome many of the daily struggles of parenting, marriage, and adulthood. I know I have made many mistakes, and I thank you for always being there to get me back on the right track. I love you. You are God's gift.

Preface

"You never know what you believe until you begin to teach your children."
- Unknown

"Children are our most valuable natural resource."
- Herbert Hoover, (1874-1964)

"If you bungle raising your children, I don't think whatever else you do well matters very much."
- Jacqueline Bouvier Kennedy Onassis, (1929-1994)

"When I approach a child, he inspires in me two sentiments; tenderness for what he is, and respect for what he may become."
- Louis Pasteur (1822-1895)

"If we don't stand for children, we don't stand for much."
- Marian Wright Edelman (1939)

Geared for Greatness, 100 Things I Taught My Children is a collection of everything I believe children must know to maximize their potential. It represents values I have personally sought to instill in my own children. Unfortunately, in our society parenting appears to be a lost art. Despite the odds, I strive to be a parent who makes a difference. Having a child does not take much effort, but raising a child is a lifelong pursuit.

There are certain principles we must ingrain in the moral fiber of our children. These principles, when utilized, will empower your child to lead a life that ascends above the level of mediocrity.

I resolutely believe that every child born has something special and unique to contribute to this world and it is our job as parents to find out what that *something* is. It is our God-given responsibility to nurture, provide for, train, and produce children who are *geared for greatness*. If you are reading this book, chances are you are a parent, or perhaps on the threshold of becoming one. You may even be someone who did not receive ideal parenting from your parents and want to use this book as a checklist for self-improvement. If you have influence in the life of a child, I believe this book will enhance that relationship.

I have found that parenting is not a mission that yields immediate results. It is, in fact, a commitment that requires lifelong perseverance, consistency, dedication, forgiveness, love, and a great deal of patience. In my judgment, there is nothing that can fully prepare you for such a significant undertaking. Hands-on experience is the best teacher.

It is imperative that you understand that you have been chosen by God to shape the life of another human being. To begin with, you are solely responsible for raising a totally unique individual. Therefore, your primary obligation in raising children who are *geared for greatness* should be to create an environment where they can flourish.

Secondly, teach by example. Anything we teach our children should first begin with us. Sadly, many fail to realize that we teach our children more by what we do rather than by what we say. It is beneficial to you and your child when you model effective principles both in word *and* deed. If you model effective principles, you will rarely have to teach them.

I am by no means an expert, but a mother of five adult children. I am certain that during my lifetime, I will have taught my children a great deal more by what I did than what I said. During my parenting years, I held onto two beliefs that helped me endure the hardships and cherish the joys of child rearing: 1) Every child is a blessing, and 2) Every child is destined for greatness.

I believe this book will be a wonderful voyage of discovery, not only for you as a parent but for you as an individual. It is my hope that you will use this as a lifelong textbook to assist you in your journey of parenting. It has taken me over thirty years of hands-on experience to write this book. It is truly an extension of my life's work. Finally, your child is the most unique, handcrafted individual on the face of this planet. Your child is fearfully and wonderfully made, knitted together in an intricate design of potential. There is no one like your child. There will never be anyone like your child. And, no one will ever be able to do what your child was created to do.

Since my child-rearing years are over, I felt that it would be prudent to publish a fourth edition. I no longer teach my children on a consistent basis, but I do remain a mentor and a coach. One of my philosophies is that you cannot raise adults; therefore, I work diligently to not give unsolicited advice. Nevertheless, I am blessed that my children and I have maintained a close connection, and they still value my input.

I have become a grandparent and am affectionately known as Grammy. The sound of it is music to my ears. My children are between the ages of 19 and 31 now, and to see them be functional, God-fearing adults is more than any parent can ask for. To watch my oldest daughter, start her own family and be an amazing loving parent is priceless. Seeing all of them etch out their own paths to success fills my heart with joy. It assures me that all my work was not in vain and that my diligence in parenting has paid off. We most definitely had our fair share of bumps and bruises, but we made it!

My oldest daughter (31) is a teacher and author of children's books. She holds a master's in education from Pepperdine University in Southern California. My oldest son (25) is a Culinary Artist and author who graduated from Le Cordon Bleu Culinary Institute. My middle daughter (23) is an amazing vocalist, songwriter, and licensed Esthetician. She is in the studio recording her freshman CD. My youngest daughter (22) is applying to several four-year universities to complete her studies in neuroscience and my youngest son (19) is working with his brother and considering a career in broadcast journalism.

In this fourth edition, I felt it necessary to add a chapter on social media and include our instructional book, Your Child's 30-day Emotional Makeover

1

Chance or Purpose?

"For you formed my inward parts; you covered me in my mother's womb. I will praise you, for I am fearfully and wonderfully made . . . my frame was not hidden from you. When I was made in secret, and skillfully wrought...."
-The Bible - Psalms 139:13 -15 (NKJV)

In 1995, I was raising four children ages 11, 5, 3, and 2. Truly convinced that my child-bearing days were over, I made an appointment with my OB/GYN doctor and requested to have my tubes tied. I attended the mandatory informational appointment, signed the consent documents and was ready to schedule the surgery. Without explanation, my doctor informed me that he was unable to tie my tubes. Five months later I found out I was pregnant and on March 13, 1996, my youngest child was born. What a wonderful addition he has been to the world. Our family would not be complete without him.

We've all heard someone refer to their child as being "an accident." An accident is defined as, "Any event that happens by chance or without known or assignable cause." This may sound a bit philosophical, but I do not believe our world operates in the realm of accidents. I believe the world we live in runs by divinely established order. Your birth was not an arbitrary incident. You were hand-chosen by God to be here.

There is a problem in existence that only your child has the power to solve. Purpose is ingrained in your genetic fiber. Who your parents are does not determine whether your life has a purpose or not. Pastor Myles Monroe, an international evangelist said, *"Maybe the only reason your parents got together was to have you."* Having your child may not have been something you planned, but I am convinced that it was God's plan. Regardless of the circumstances surrounding the conception of a child, no child is a mistake.

GEARED FOR GREATNESS

Every life was created by divine design.

Teach your child that his/her life has significant value.

2

Incredible Gift

"Genius is one percent inspiration and 99% perspiration."
- Thomas Alva Edison (1847-1931)

"Behold, children are a heritage from the Lord. The fruit of the womb is a reward."- The Bible - Psalms 127:3-4 (NKJV)

Ludwig van Beethoven (Composer), Albert Einstein (Theory of Relativity), Dr. Benjamin Carson (Pediatric Brain Surgeon), Helen Keller (Blind Author/Educator) and many others, were all extremely gifted children who were considered academically inept according to conventional educational standards. Yet, these individuals have left an indelible mark on the forward progress of this nation and abroad.

Consider the idea that every child is born a genius. Genius is defined as, "A single strongly marked capacity, extraordinary intellectual power manifested in creative activity, *a gift*." Children are a gift waiting to be unwrapped. Some gifts in children are very evident from the start and other gifts are progressively revealed. Make it your assignment to discover your child's innate gift. Once they are identified and developed, your child can become a person of great significance in this world. Your child's gift in operation will enable him/her to effectively pursue his/her purpose and destiny.

Everyone is born with a mission to fulfill in life. At conception, thousands of sperm are released towards one egg, but only one is generally allowed to fertilize and grow. Statistically, there are millions of abortions each year. Therefore, if your child made it to this earth then he/she has something important and specific to accomplish. Your child is not here just to occupy space or waste time.

Teach your child that gift(s) are innate endowments given by God to fully equip a person to effect change in this world.

3

Be the First to Say Hello

Polite people always speak first! Rudeness should never be tolerated. One of the first things I made my children do when they got up in the morning was speak. My grandfather was a stickler for greeting one another in the morning. When I failed to do so, he would say, "Did you sleep with me last night?" He was saying, if this is the first time you have seen me today say, "Hello."

Don't wait for someone to speak to you first. I have made it my mission in life to be the resident greeter. No matter where I go, it is my responsibility to spread good cheer. Speaking first demonstrates that you take the initiative to create a pleasant environment.

Teach your child the art of saying hello.

4

Don't Break Rank

Life is a battle. It is not for the weak, weary or faint of heart. It takes stalwart fortitude and obstinate strength to survive in the world today. One of the worst things a soldier can do in the heat of battle is to break rank. Lives are hanging in the balance. People depend on soldiers to remain steadfast, able, and ready to fulfill their responsibilities and to be consistent in their duties.

Teach your child to never yield to defeat; stay in position like a soldier; respect the authority of the person in charge and keep his/her eyes on winning the battle.

5

The Lost Art of Marriage

"Even if there are two points of view, agree to have one direction."
- Pastor Charles Martin (1967 -)

"A successful marriage requires falling in love many times, always with the same person." - Mignon McLaughlin *(1913-1983)*

"In a time when nothing is more certain than change, the commitment of two people to one another has become difficult and rare. Yet, by its scarcity, the beauty and value of this exchange have only been enhanced." - Unknown

Marriage is a wonderful institution. It truly is a commitment that takes careful consideration. Its success depends not only on finding the perfect mate but striving to be the perfect mate. Children generally tend to choose mates that have qualities very like the parent of the opposite sex. Considering this fact, I strive every day to be a good role model for my children. I consistently convey to them, "I am the standard by which you live." I will never require anything of them that I am not willing to do myself. I painstakingly make every effort to emulate the type of person I want my sons to spend the rest of their lives with, and I teach my daughters how to exude the character of an excellent wife. Teach your child how much you love him/her by your willingness to be a good example before him/her.

    In marriage, you may not always be in a state of constant agreement but you can always agree to disagree. If two people are willing to give equally, with the understanding that at times one person may have to give more than the other, then it can work. Both husband and wife must be willing to sacrifice for the greater good. In marriage, you must find what works best for the marriage and the family not just for the individual.

GEARED FOR GREATNESS

Teach your child that marriage must include the ability to forgive, to love, to support, to honor, to give, to be present, to compromise, to provide for and to encourage each other.

What we speak into our lives and the lives of our children is crucial.

As you engage in speaking the words of affirmation listed below, call every one of your children by name. I encourage you to be honest in answering every question. We can only change the things we are willing to acknowledge or confront. Therefore, I have included affirmations and thought-provoking questions throughout this book to aid you in gearing your child for greatness.

Affirmation #1

- Regardless of the circumstances surrounding my child's birth, I declare my child is a gift from God.

- I declare the world is making room for my child's gift(s).

- I declare my child is strong, courageous, and responsible and will greatly impact his/her generation.

- I declare I am alert and attentive to recognize my child's gift(s).

- I declare I will do everything I can to give my child the opportunity to excel in his/her gift.

- I declare my child embraces the art of *saying hello* first when in the presence of people.

- I declare I will be an example for my child to follow.

GEARED FOR GREATNESS

Questions

What have I learned from the last few chapters?
(Chance or Purpose? Incredible Gift; Be the First to Say Hello; Don't Break Rank; The Lost Art of Marriage)

Where can I improve?

From observation, what is my child's predominant gift?

What can I do to develop my child's gift?

6

Lead, Don't Follow

"Be an opener of doors for such as come after thee."
- Ralph Waldo Emerson (1803-1882)

Whether born with a natural ability to lead or not, leadership skills need to be developed in every child. If children learn to lead and take command of their environment, they are less apt to follow the crowd. Rick Warren, the author of the book, *A Purpose Driven Life,* said, *"If you follow the crowd you eventually get lost in it."*

Many children get into trouble or cower under peer pressure because they are imitating or following someone else. Developing your child's leadership skills will give him/her confidence to stand in front and pave the way.

Teach your child the principles of effective leadership.

7

Never Too Busy to Listen

"Sometimes we are so busy making a living that we forget to make a life." - John Wooden (1910- 2010)

You must begin if you haven't already done so, to make up your mind that there is nothing more important than your responsibility of parenting. We as parents think everything else is so important and that things demand our immediate attention or undying commitment right now. In many cases, these demands turn out to be time wasters and major distractions from what should be our focus—our children. Usually, the things we commit to outside of our family responsibilities will not make an eternal impact on our lives or the lives of others. Spend your time wisely.

Regardless of what I am doing and how important it may seem to me, it is imperative I set time aside daily to listen to the sometimes annoying and trivial questions that are asked of me by my children. I've come to understand that every question deserves an answer. If you don't answer your child's questions, someone else will. That someone may or may not be your ideal choice. Children, without question, equate love with time and attention. The more time you give a child, the more loved they feel. Just as a farmer plants seeds and nurtures them with the necessary ingredients to produce a maximum harvest, so must we nurture the lives of our children. It has been said, "Children don't want your presents, they want your presence."

Time is swiftly moving and can never be replaced. Don't live your life in a state of constant regret because you allowed yourself to get weighed down with things that were not producing an eternal return. There is nothing more pressing than your child's future. You have 18 years to raise your child, impart wisdom and lend a listening ear. Hopefully, your child

GEARED FOR GREATNESS

will welcome your continued presence past them turning 18 so you can spend a lifetime enjoying the fruits of your labor.

Teach your child how much you love them by spending quality time with him/her.

8

Hugs and Kisses Last a Lifetime

"A warm heart is medicine for the soul."
-Yvonne Camper (1964 -)

Affection is a basic human necessity that people require from the cradle to the grave. There is nothing more nurturing than the touch and feel of another human being. An adequate amount of love and affection gives children the ability to distinguish between healthy and unhealthy affection. It gives them a sense of being, increases their self-esteem, and teaches them to be affectionate and loving individuals. Hugs and kisses last a lifetime and forge a bond that cannot be broken—even by the grave.

Teach your child not to let life make him/her cold-hearted and to always keep a warm heart.

9

Heart of Compassion

"Let my heart be broken with the things that break the heart of God." -Bob Pierce (Founder of World Vision, est. 1950)

"How far you go in life depends on you being tender with the young, compassionate with the aged, sympathetic with the striving and tolerant of the weak and strong. Because someday in life you will be these." - George Washington Carver (1864 -1943)

Compassion is defined as, "Sorrow for another's suffering or misfortune." We live in a self-centered, *"me-istic"* society. Everything revolves around what we need, what we want, and what affects us. Rarely are we stirred by the plight of others. In recent times, the greatest demonstrations of compassion by our society followed the tragedies of 9/11 and Hurricane Katrina. It is a sad state of affairs when we are only moved to care for the less fortunate in times of tragedy.

There is nothing that warms my heart more than seeing my older children take care of their younger siblings. I have taught my children that not only are they responsible for themselves but it is also their God-given duty to be mindful of those entrusted into their care. Caring for others teaches a child that there is a world outside of himself/herself, and that there are many in need of a human touch. You must make every effort and seize every opportunity to nurture a heart of compassion in your child.

Instead of allowing the "me, myself, and I" syndrome to operate in your child, teach him/her to live by the unselfish motto, "Each one can reach one."

10

Parenting Is Seasonal

You will not be changing diapers, warming bottles, helping with homework and being a taxi all your life. Enjoy the process of parenting. Cherish the journey. Just as life is seasonal, so is parenting. Learn to change with the seasons.

One of the greatest things a parent can do for a child is to allow him/her room to grow up. Parents will find that it is also one of the hardest things to do! We must know when it is time to *let go*. The purpose of parenting will always be to teach your child to be self-governing. Trust yourself enough to know that what you instilled in your child will serve him/her well.

Teach your child that you trust him/her enough to allow him/her to become the extraordinary individual he/she was designed to be.

11

Be Responsible

Responsibility defined is, "The act of being answerable, reliable, or dependable." Making a child accountable for their own behavior gives them the ability to respond appropriately to his/her environment. By far, the most painful part of teaching a child responsibility is allowing them to suffer the consequences of their own behaviors. Constantly rescuing a child creates an unhealthy expectation that no matter what decisions he/she makes, someone will be there to fix whatever damages were incurred.

A child without responsibility loses the ability to command their environment; the child may develop an unconscious tendency to blame others for his/her failures. The habit of blaming others relieves you from personal responsibility and empowers other people to determine your future.

Teach your child that making excuses for failures makes them powerless and unable to create the life that they desire.

Affirmation #2

- I declare my child is strong and will not get lost in the sea of peer pressure.

- I declare my child will become a responsible adult and will contribute greatly to the betterment of humanity.

- I declare my child has a heart of compassion and is not selfish, self-centered, or self-absorbed.

- I declare my child is *"response-able"* and takes personal responsibility for his/her behavior.

- I declare my child will become a well-balanced and stable adult.

- I declare I am never too busy to spend time with, talk to, play with, or listen to my child.

- I declare I give my child the affection due him/her and that my child will never have to go elsewhere to be emotionally fulfilled.

- I declare I am attentive and readily accessible to my child.

Questions

What have I learned from the last few chapters?
(Lead, Don't Follow; Never Too Busy to Listen; Hugs and Kisses Last a Lifetime; A Heart of Compassion; Parenting Is Seasonal; Be Responsible)

How can I demonstrate a heart of compassion to my child?

What can I do to develop leadership skills in my child?

What can I do to show my child more love and affection?

12

The Big Brute

Encouraging physical retaliation when angry, is literally teaching your child the most barbaric form of communication. Obviously, this is something you don't want to do. Granted, there are times when you must physically defend yourself but brute force should never be your first response.

When I was younger, fighting was always my first response to everything. One day, I was looking through some of my old family photos, and I came across a picture that was taken at summer camp when I was about ten years old. One of the things written on the back of the photo by a camp counselor read, "Yvonne, learn to talk with your mouth and not your hands."

To say the least, I was tickled pink because I had no recollection of the event and certainly, I have learned since that time to *not* communicate with my hands. Learning to be an effective fighter using intellect and reason is far better than using fisticuffs. One tactic I have learned in this type of situation is knowing when to walk away and to realize at what point a verbal disagreement is no longer productive.

Teach your child that physical fighting is not effective in resolving conflict.

13

Be A Valuable Employee

Our culture is saturated with people who want something for nothing. Whether scooping ice cream or running a major corporation, it is important to take pride in what you do. I've been in the workforce for many years, and I have watched the level of commitment and excellence greatly diminish. Employers these days take a huge risk when hiring people. They understand all too well that good employees are very difficult to come by these days.

Having dreams and aspirations of one day owning your own company is great, but first, learn to be a good employee. If you cannot be a good employee at someone else's company, you will never be able to effectively run your own company.

Sure, everyone would prefer to start at the top in business, instead of working their way up from the bottom. But keep in mind that there is no building on earth that has ever been built from the top down. Everything worthwhile begins on the ground floor and even that must be built upon a sturdy foundation. Dave Thomas, the founder of Wendy's hamburger chain, started as a busboy and ended up owning a multi-billion-dollar corporation. If you have been given a job, perform it to the best of your ability. Teach your child not to cut corners.

Teach him/her to be dependable, reliable, and efficient at work.

14

Focus - The Key to Success

"The greatest thing a man can do in this world is to make the most possible out of the stuff that has been given him. This is success, and there is no other."-
Orison Swett Marden (1850 -1924)

Focus is concentrated power. Staying focused is crucial to successful endeavors. Keep a snapshot of your goals seared in the vaults of your mind. It gives you the ability to see something from inception to implementation. It is better to not start a task at all than to start it and not complete it. Plan to finish.

Many people start projects and never see them through to completion. Oftentimes, this is because they hit a roadblock or get stuck. One of the key ingredients of success is identifying your limitations and following through on the things that you know you can complete.

Teach your child to ask for assistance in areas where he/she experiences limitations or has a lack of knowledge. This will enable him/her to become a finisher in life. Focus is a must!

15

The Power of Self-Control

*"But the fruit of the spirit is love, joy, peace, longsuffering, kindness, goodness, faithfulness, gentleness, **self-control**. Against such there is no law."* -The Bible - Galatians 5:22-23 (NKJV)

Self-control defined is, "The aptitude to deduce what your response will be to any given stimulus." Basically, it is thinking before you react. Exercising self-control is just as crucial to your child's development as learning to read. Lack of self-control and discipline is the bedrock of many a failure. It is virtually impossible for a person out of control to be effective in anything they strive to do. We all know from our own personal experiences or those of others that acting on impulse can be quite dangerous and the consequences can be extremely costly.

Controlling one's behavior and emotions at times can be quite difficult, depending on the magnitude of the stimulus. But, it is not an impossible task. Stephen Covey says, "Between every action there is a space in time to determine what the reaction or response is going to be." Teach your child to recognize and utilize *that* space in time to respond by thought rather than react by impulse.

Teach your child to choose behavior that will produce favorable outcomes.

16

Mind Your Manners

We all wish our children were born with good manners. Unfortunately, the odds of this happening are extremely rare. Manners must be taught. They are one of the most essential elements of a child's social success. Experts say the following about manners:

Correction

Refrain from open rebuke if possible. Understand the purpose of correction is for improvement, not embarrassment.

Mistakes

Depending on the age of your child, you must correct him/her consistently and constantly, accepting the fact it will not be an overnight process.

Be Positive

Instead of consistently telling your child what is wrong, tell him/her what is appropriate and acceptable. For example, show your child what you want him/her to do. Strive to be a good model. In addition, save your scolding for major infractions and not minor ones. Eventually, your child will get it.

Teach your child that good manners are imperative to social success.

Affirmation #3

- I declare my child is caring and sensitive to the needs of others.

- I declare my child is focused and able to complete all tasks with excellence.

- I declare my child is extremely hard-working and demonstrates excellence in everything he/she puts his/her hands to.

- I declare my child handles all life's issues with the spirit of self-control and is not physically or verbally out of control with his/her responses.

- I declare that as a parent, I first lead by example.

- I declare that as a parent, I operate in the spirit of self-control.

- I declare I have an excellent work ethic, and I can teach my child to have an excellent work ethic as well.

Questions

What have I learned from the past few chapters?
(The Big Brute; Be A Valuable Employee; Focus: The Key to Success; The Power of Self-Control; Mind Your Manners)

Where can I improve?

What can I do to instill a good work ethic in my child?

What can I do to help my child focus better?

Do I feel I am a good example for my child? If not, what can I do to change that perception?

17

Speak Up!

"From the mouths of little children and infants, you have built a fortress against your opponents to silence the enemy and the avenger."- The Bible - Psalms 8:2 (God's Word Translation)

I do not believe the adage, "Children should be seen and not heard." Children have a lot to say and are full of wisdom. There are many things my children have said to me that I truly value. It is a rewarding process when you permit your child the privilege of expressing his/her feelings. Within boundaries, it is perfectly healthy for a child to state what he/she feels about certain situations. Of course, I do not allow my children to be disrespectful when doing so. Expression without respect is a fine line that needs to be taught and practiced.

I have learned that feelings are neither right nor wrong. They are just feelings. A child has feelings just as adults do. Speaking up teaches a child how to communicate even in conflict. By allowing a child this type of interaction, his/her communication skills are sharpened. One of the main reasons people fail or do not achieve the status in life that they would like to achieve is due to ineffective communication.

Parents who are good communicators usually raise children who are good communicators. Sadly, the opposite is also true concerning poor communication. Good communication is the center of every successful relationship. Where communication is lacking, the destruction of families, businesses, and friendships are inevitable. Engaging in effective communication is not just verbal; it involves the whole being. It includes body language, active listening, tone, and emotion. One of the ways we teach our children to communicate is by communicating with them, and allowing them full expression, both verbal and emotional.

Teach your child the value of communicating and to avoid the pitfalls of holding things inside.

18

The Rewards of Discipline

"He who spares his rod hates his son, but he who loves him disciplines him promptly." -The Bible - Proverbs 13:24 (NKJV)

Discipline has its rewards. Even though many, currently, oppose physical discipline, I feel it is necessary at times. I would rather raise my children than have my children raise me because I failed to do my job. Physical discipline is not appropriate in every case. There are times when children, like adults, make mistakes. Mistakes should be treated as such. The punishment should fit the crime, so to speak.

Having disciplined my children, I am able to enjoy being with them, instead of feeling as if their presence is a burden or even worse—a threat. I believe that the teenage years do not have to be tumultuous. Not all change is cataclysmic. I do want to give a word of caution though—never apply physical discipline out of frustration or anger.

The book of Proverbs in the Bible says, "A good son makes his mother happy." With proper discipline, children can lead a productive and fruitful life. Parental discipline teaches a child how to respect authority and respond to it appropriately.

Some disciplinary methods I use in lieu of physical discipline:

- Standing in the corner.
- Time-out.
- Writing standards.
- Research and report writing.
- Going to bed early.
- Taking away favorite things.
- Not allowed to leave the house.
- Prohibiting videos, games, or cell phone usage.

The rewards of discipline:

- It develops a teachable spirit.
- Kills the spirit of rebellion.
- Teaches a child respect for authority.
- Gives a child the ability to lead a productive life and not spend it learning "hard" lessons because of their failure to listen.
- Discipline enables a child to keep solid and healthy relationships with his/her parents.

Teach your child that the goal of parental discipline is self-discipline.

19

The Power of Family and Friends

"To us, family means putting your arms around each other and being there."-
Barbara Bush, (1925-)

"A man who has friends must himself be friendly…"
-The Bible - Proverbs 18:24 (NKJV)

Family, in my opinion, is the most significant entity in the world. It is where we get our identity, our sense of importance, love, and acceptance for us to grow and mature. Family is not just a group of people who are related by bloodline but can also be people not related and with whom a deep, intimate connection is shared.

There are times when natural families are not as instrumental in our lives as we would have hoped or envisioned. But life always seems to send someone to replace what we believe we have lost. Learn to appreciate the *"family"* in your life. Cherish family. Respect family. Spend time with family. Love and have fun with family. Teach your child to be proud of the family that he/she has been given, both related and unrelated.

Friendships are just as vital as your family. The Bible says David's and Jonathan's hearts were "knitted together." They possessed a friendship that surpassed even the grave. Regrettably, in our society, friendship is not valued the way it used to be.
People tend to only be loyal to themselves.

Share the value and benefit of true friendship with your child by example. Teach your child to be the kind of friend he/she would like to have and instruct him/her that people are an invaluable resource that cannot be replaced.

GEARED FOR GREATNESS

At times when I am feeling low,
I hear from a friend and then
My worries start to go away
And I am on the mend.

In spite, of all that doctors know,
And their studies never end,
The best cure of all when spirits fall
Is a kind note from a friend.
– John Wooden

20

My, How Time Flies

"If you're burning the candle at both ends, you're not as bright as you think you are." - Unknown

Effectively learning to manage time and avoid procrastination is one of the greatest lessons that your child can learn. Be on time to work, school, your place of worship, and every appointment. Wasting another person's time is just like wasting their money. Time is a valuable commodity. Remember the old saying, "Time will tell." It's true. Time reveals much over a long period. We all hope to stand the test of time.

Teach your child to respect time at an early age and to always arrive a few minutes early to avoid being late.

21

The Value of Loyalty

Loyalty is an unswerving allegiance to what we believe. Loyalty is something that cannot be bought, only exemplified. Faithfulness, dedication, and commitment are the things that distinguish the common from the uncommon and mediocrity from excellence. It is our mandate as parents to teach our children to be loyal to God, loyal to your country, loyal to your family and loyal to your friends.

Affirmation #4

- I declare my child is not afraid to express himself/herself and is learning that verbal expression is okay when done in a respectful manner.

- I declare my child is learning to be a good friend.

- I declare my child is loyal in relationships.

- I declare my child has healthy relationships and all unhealthy relationships are dissolved.

- I declare I teach my child how to effectively manage his/her time.

- I declare I teach my child to respect other people's time.

- I declare I teach my child the benefit of arriving a few minutes early to scheduled appointments, school, and work.

- I declare I teach my child the gift of expression, and I am not afraid to allow my child to express dissatisfaction, anger, sadness, or pain in my presence.

- I declare I am consistent and fair in my discipline.

- I declare I teach my child by example and instruct the value of family, friendship, and loyalty.

Questions

What have I learned from the last few chapters?
(Speak Out! The Rewards Of Discipline; The Power Of Family And Friends; My How Time Flies; The Value Of Loyalty)

Where can I improve?

Do I allow my child the forum to express himself/herself freely? If not, am I willing to change and allow my child to express freely without disrespect?

What can I do to teach my child the value of loyalty and friendship?

22

Don't Compromise Who You Are

"To thine own self be true, and it must follow, as the night the day, thou canst not be false to any man." - Shakespeare (1564-1616)

Compromise is defined as, "to weaken." You can never compromise your beliefs without compromising who you are. Stick to your guns and stand firm on what you believe. Teach your child to be true to his/her most excellent self. Most parents make a gallant effort to instill good morals and character into their children. However, if life takes a turn that challenges their belief system, they can begin to question their stance. I heard one parent tell a child, "Don't let someone rip out of you in a moment what I spent a lifetime putting into you."

That is why we must stand as vigilant warriors and correct every area where we see our child giving in to compromise. In so doing, we are fortifying the walls and building up a defense that is unable to be penetrated.

Teach your child to stand firm on his/her beliefs and not be swayed by the opinion of others.

23

Never Say Can't

Can't defined implies, "That a person is unable to affect an outcome normally under his/her control, or the inability to produce." It is a word that will stop you dead in your tracks and prohibit you from being all you can be. The fact is, you possess a God-given ability. You can do anything! I love this poem by the people's poet, Edgar A. Guest (1881-1959):

Can't is the worst word that's written or spoken:
Doing more harm here than slander and lies;
On it is many a strong spirit broken,
It springs from the lips of the thoughtless each morning
And robs us of courage we need through the day
And laughs when we falter and fall by the way.
Can't is the father of a feeble endeavor
The parent of terror and half-hearted work;
It weakens the efforts of artisans clear,
And makes of the toiler an indolent shirk
It poisons the soul of man with a vision
It stifles in infancy many a plan
It greets honest toiling with open derision
And mocks at the hopes and the dreams of a man.
Can't is a word none should speak without blushing;
To utter it should be a symbol of shame
Ambition and courage, it daily is crushing
It blights a man's purpose and shortens his aim
Despise it with all of your hatred of error
Arm against it as a creature of terror
And all that you dream of you some day, shall gain
Can't is a word that is foe to ambition
An enemy ambushed to shatter your will

GEARED FOR GREATNESS

*Its prey is forever the man with a mission
And bows but to courage and patience and skill
Hate it, with hatred that's deep and undying
For once it is welcomed 'twill break any man:
Whatever the goal you are seeking, keep trying
And answer this demon by saying "I can."*

24

In His Image

"So, God created man in His own image…"
-The Bible - Genesis 1:27 (NKJV)

While on this earth, we are the visual expression of God. We are His voice, His ears, His hands, and His feet. As God's representatives on this earth, we must take on His good will and character. If anything, *"good"* is going to happen on this earth, it is going to happen through you.

God is the most productive, powerful, and creative being in the universe. He is immovable, unshakable, steadfast and resolute in everything He does. He is faithful, merciful, kind, generous, forgiving, loving, and patient. He is a wonderful counselor, a patient ear, and an unwavering friend.

Teach your child that the most awesome thing about him/her is that he/she is created in **GOD'S IMAGE**.

25

Soar with Eagles

"A man's reach should exceed his grasp or what's a heaven for?"
-Robert Browning (1812-1889)

Liberty begins in the mind. If you want your child to reign with kings, then teach him/her how to walk with kings. Most of a child's outlook on life is based on what he/she is exposed to during his/her childhood. Many children don't learn to live superior lives simply because they never see superior lives being lived out in front of them. If circumstances prevent you from exposing your child to the best life must offer, the library is a wonderful resource. It is always available and free of charge. A library card is a passport to your child's future. Utilizing libraries can expose your child to other countries, cultures, and people they may never have the opportunity to see or meet. Teach your child the only limitations in life are the ones he/she puts on himself/herself.

26

Dare to Be Great

"The difference between greatness and mediocrity is often how an individual views a mistake."
-Nelson Boswell (1740-1795)

"The price of greatness is responsibility."
-Sir Winston Churchill (1874-1965)

"A great man is always willing to be little."
- Ralph Waldo Emerson (1803-1882)

"There are countless ways of achieving greatness, but any road to achieving one's maximum potential must be built on a bed-rock of respect for the individual, a commitment to excellence and a rejection of mediocrity."
-Buck Rogers (Fictional Character–1928)

Embedded in every individual is the power to reach greatness. Becoming great or not depends on one's ability to bring forth the greatness within. People of greatness possess unyielding courage. They have an unstoppable ability to overcome adversity and an undaunted passion for what they believe in. The individuals who achieve greatness in our society are those who dare to be different, dare to take risks and dare to be fearless!

As parents, it is our responsibility to unlock the greatness locked within our children. If we teach them to light the torch, they will soon be able to carry it. Teach your child he/she determines his/her own destiny and he/she has the power within to become a great person. A great person does great things!

Affirmation #5

- I declare my child is strong in his/her convictions.

- I declare my child does not waiver in what he/she believes.

- I declare my child will not make a habit of saying the words "*I can't.*" But rather, my child will possess a heart full of courage.

- I declare my child is willing to put in the work to be great and rise above mediocrity.

- I declare I am strong in my convictions and do not compromise my beliefs.

- I declare my child and I are created in the image of God; therefore, we can do anything that we set our hearts to do.

- I declare I am consistently creating an environment where my child can flourish and tap into his/her greatness.

Questions

What have I learned in the past few chapters?
(Don't Compromise Who You Are; Never Say Can't; In His Image; Soar with Eagles; Dare to Be Great)

Where can I improve?

Where in my life have I compromised and what am I willing to do to get back to my personal convictions?

What attributes of God do I see in myself?

What attributes of God do I see in my child?

27

Munificent Giving

"Think of giving not as a duty but as a privilege."
-John D. Rockefeller, Jr. (1874-1960)

"What we have done for ourselves alone dies with us; what we have done for others and the world remains and is immortal."
- Albert Pikes (1809-1891)

Munificence is the act of giving generously or lavishly. Generosity is something that we all practice from time to time. But that is not the giving I am referring to. I am referring to the giving that is lavish and sacrificial. We are all busy and our plates are full but it is important to remember a life without giving is an empty life. I have vowed personally to leave this world empty and spent of all. Everything that was placed in me during my lifetime will be dispensed into the lives of others before I breathe my last breath. Developing a generous soul is something that is progressively obtained. Generosity must be practiced consistently and be weaved into day to day tasks and activities.

Give freely of yourself, your time, and your resources to those who have an earnest need, especially when you are financially able to do so. If you have been given much, you must give much. In today's vernacular, it's called *paying it forward*. Giving should never be motivated by selfish ambitions but rather out of the abundance of a benevolent heart. When giving is done with the expectation that something is owed, the flow of giving will always be metered by a response or reaction. One rarely gathers the harvest of giving in the same field it was planted. But the law of sowing and reaping will ensure the harvest is coming!

Teach your child it is an honor to be able to give sacrificially.

28

Encourage Creativity

"I must study politics and war that my sons may have liberty to study mathematics and philosophy. My sons ought to study mathematics, philosophy, geography, natural history, naval architecture, navigation, commerce and agriculture in order to give their children a right to study painting, poetry, music, architecture, statuary, tapestry and porcelain."
- John Adams, (1735-1826)

True creativity stimulates the mind, will, and emotions. Most creative thinkers are innately articulate, adaptable, innovative, imaginative, detailed, and elaborate in their ability to produce. Creativity is seeing what no one else sees, thinking what no else has thought and doing what no one else has dared to do. Encourage independent thinking and creativity in your child.

One of the biggest deficiencies in our educational system was the removal of the art programs. I have observed that children with artistic abilities tend to struggle in conventional educational systems. In my opinion, the lack of creative expression in the classroom is one reason there has been an astronomical rise in childhood attention deficit disorders. Artistic outlets allow students the ability to release creative energy, which in turn can reduce the pressure of the day-to-day monotony of reading, writing, and arithmetic.

Teach your child artistic expression is necessary for spiritual and emotional growth and well-being.

29

Wisdom Is the Principal Thing

"Wisdom is the principal thing; therefore, get wisdom…"
-The Bible - Proverbs 4:7 (KJV)

Wisdom defined is, "The ability to discern inner qualities and relationships—insight; good sense—judgment." Wisdom gives us the capability to recognize truth and apply it to our daily life. Wisdom in action makes everything around us run more efficiently, produces luminosity of life, superior actions, more excellent endeavors and effective strategies by which we can bring about change in our lives.

Wisdom is the aptitude to perceive the big picture and understand it. It is not always acquired from the vaults of academic achievement or from a high society pedigree. It can be found in every class of society. Earthly wisdom can be found in countless resources.

Wisdom from above *only* emanates from the throne of God and a prudent man will pray to Him for it. A fool will refuse to seek a source higher than himself.

Teach your child to admit when he/she does not know everything. When one lacks wisdom, it is okay to ask for help on a matter. A wise man seeks counsel.

30

The Power of Forgiveness

Forgiveness defined is, "To grant relief of payment, pardon, excuse, release, the act of releasing someone for past hurts or disappointments." Forgiveness is not an easy *thing to bestow*. But it is an *essential* thing if you are going to live a life that is fruitful and effective. Nothing blocks the creative flow of life more than *un-forgiveness*.

I am convinced un-forgiveness is the root of all "*dis-eases*." It produces a spirit of bitterness, resentment and hatred. It eats away at you like cancer. Refusing to forgive someone hurts you, not the person responsible for hurting you. *Un-forgiveness* destroys relationships and lives and deactivates our God-given abilities.

When we refuse to forgive, we are telling God that Jesus' death on the cross was not enough. We must understand that God's grace is sufficient for any wrong that was ever done to us. It is impossible to possess all that the future has in store for you when you are stuck in the past.

Teach your child the beauty of forgiveness and to forgive others for the sake of his/her own well-being.

31

Be Thankful

Stop and smell the roses!" Learn that the art of being thankful requires the ability to embrace the quality and worth of your life. It is accepting that you are exactly where you are supposed to be at this moment. This includes the good, the bad, and the ugly. There is always something to be thankful for, even if it is just one small thing in this life. Life is a symphony of experiences. We take so many things in life for granted. Learning to see the beauty in small things is a quality long forgotten.

As a society, we seldom stop to think about how much we must be thankful for in life. Thanksgiving should be a daily mindset and not a holiday celebrated just once a year. Being grateful means that you have learned the value of acceptance and that there are some things you will never be able to change.

Be sensitive to the people around you. There is always someone who has a problem worse than your own problem. Be grateful that things in your life are not as bad as they could be. Take stock of the good things that are going on in your life. Sometimes, circumstances come into our lives to challenge the "status quo." Always be ready for *that* challenge. Take joy in the small things. When we focus on loss, we underestimate what we still possess. Teach your child to be thankful for the intangible things in life as well as the tangible. Teach your child to say thank you out loud.

Affirmation #6

- I declare my child learns how to forgive and does not harbor bitterness.

- I declare my child is creative and possesses wisdom for every decision made in life.

- I declare my child's future spouse will be chosen by God.

- I declare my child will learn to effectively communicate in every situation.

- I declare I have a heart of forgiveness and I am not harboring resentment, bitterness or un-forgiveness towards any person living or dead.

- I declare I will consistently ask God for wisdom in raising the child or children He has given me.

- I declare I consistently look for creative ways to teach my child and create environments where my child can flourish.

- I declare if I am married, I successfully teach my child the value and blessings of marriage by example. If I am not married, I teach my child through the Word of God (the Bible) the principles of relationships and what a good marriage looks like through the eyes of God.

- I declare my child will have a successful marriage.

Questions

What have I learned from the last few chapters?
(Munificent Giving; Encourage Creativity; Wisdom Is the Principal Thing; The Power of Forgiveness; Be Thankful)

Where can I improve?

Is there anyone in my life (living or dead) who I have not forgiven? If so, am I willing to begin the process of forgiveness? List the people you need to forgive.
1.
2.
3.
4.
5.
6.
7.
8.
9.
10.

What areas in my life do I need wisdom?

Prayer of Forgiveness

I declare every person (living or dead) who I have not forgiven is being released by me, at this moment. I declare there is nothing these people owe me or have to repay me and I release all of them now from all wrong-doing. I also declare I forgive myself for harboring bitterness, resentment, anger, hatred and pain. This day I am healed from betrayal and disappointment. I am free from all the effects of un-forgiveness.

32

The Gift of Closure

Closure is the one event that can extract you from the jaws of your past and catapult you into the winds of your destiny. Many times, in life, plans don't work out. That does not mean that you must suffer for the rest of your life. If it didn't happen, maybe it wasn't supposed to happen. Learning to close a chapter and walk away from your plans can take lots of practice.

I have learned that every experience, every failure, and every success is a *"potter's wheel experience."* An experience that continuously shapes us into who we are destined to become. These experiences tend to open doors to the future. Yet, you are the only one who has the power to walk through those doors. Regret of past experiences can turn into a horrible monster keeping you anchored and chained to the past.

Teach your child to resolve personal issues and put those issues to rest. There are circumstances in life that require people to move on and get over them! Including, but certainly not limited to: a lost relationship, an unfulfilled dream or a bad decision. Peace is captured in just letting it go, forgetting those things which are behind us and pressing forward to those things which eagerly lie ahead.

Teach your child to look ahead and not get trapped in viewing life through a rear-view mirror.

33

Two Are Better Than One

Successful empires are not built on the back of one individual but rather on the shoulders of a multitude of competent individuals. No one person possesses enough within to accomplish everything necessary in this thing we call life.

Everyone needs a helping hand from time to time. God is so wise. He prepared a way for us by embedding what we would need along the way, into the lives of other people. I never cultivate the idea in my children that their strength and ability alone is sufficient. *Everybody* needs help.

Teach your child that asking for help is a sign of strength and maturity.

34

Count Your Blessings

"Even lilies grow in rugged terrain."
- Charles Stanley (1932-)

"Life throws you many curve balls, but if you hang in there, you just might learn how to hit a few."
- Queen Latifah (1970 -)

I remember when I was a child there was a picture that hung in our bathroom that read, *"When life gives you lemons, make lemonade."* In life, it is not *what* happens to you that matters. It is *what* you do with *what* happens to you that counts. It is not *where* you start that matters. It is *where* you finish. There is something to be grateful for even in the most insignificant things. Obstacles are not setbacks, just changes in direction. It is the wind at the back that propels a boat forward.

Teach your child to remember that light shines through even the smallest cracks and to count all blessings both small and large.

35

Pay Attention to Details

Details are the small elements that collectively constitute a work of art. One thread can unravel an entire sweater. It is a collection of brush strokes that create a beautiful painting. It is the single threads of a tapestry that creates an exquisite masterpiece. Contrary to what many believe, it is not the big things that destroy deals, relationships or businesses. But rather, the little things that are so easily overlooked. It is the minute details not addressed due to not taking the necessary time to do so, that eventually cause things to deteriorate. This requires taking time to notice the little things. If left unattended one crack in a dam can cause the entire dam to burst wide open!

Teach your child to pay attention to details.

36

Don't Over-Stimulate Your Child

Our society is always on the go! Staying home and relaxing is a lost art these days. Many parents sit their children down in front of the television, give them video games and allow them to do a multitude of seemingly self-governing activities just to keep them occupied. These same children seldom ever learn the discipline and rewards of just sitting still and doing absolutely nothing.

With the advent of social media and the internet, it is more important than ever that we don't allow our children to suck up unfiltered information. It will be important in the long run to remind your children that silence is golden and that every waking hour does not have to be filled with an activity.

Teach your child some of the deepest truths are only revealed in the dead of silence.

Affirmation #7

- I declare my child forgets the past and embraces the future.

- I declare my child knows when to ask for help.

- I declare my child has a grateful heart and looks for the blessing in everything.

- I declare my child pays attention to details.

- I declare my child appreciates the art of sitting still and self-reflection.

- I declare I let go of everything in my past that may be hindering my future.

- I declare I can ask for help when it is necessary.

- I declare I pay attention to details.

GEARED FOR GREATNESS

Questions

What have I learned in the past few chapters?
(The Gift of Closure; Two Are Better Than One; Count Your Blessings; Pay Attention to Details; Don't Over-Stimulate Your Child)

Where can I improve?

What can I do to assist my child in having a grateful heart and being more appreciative?

What activities do I need to limit in order not to over-stimulate my child?

37

Failure and Adversity

"Failure is not trying."
- James Damon Every (1964 -)

"Failure is not the falling down but the staying down…"
- Chinese Proverb

"Adversity never makes or breaks a person; it only reveals their true character."
- Martin Luther (1483-1546)

Failure is not the end of the world and adversity is inevitable. Learning to deal with failure and loss will give your child a significant edge in life. Teach your child that there are many benefits to what we term as failure. Failure breeds perseverance, perfection, new insight and a fresh start. If you are ever going to strive to do something great, failure is inevitable and part of the process. When we fail, we must put it behind us and move on. Thomas Alva Edison failed a multitude of times before he invented the light bulb.

The winds of adversity never cease to rage. Adversity is the common thread that binds humanity together. John F. Kennedy, Jr., when questioned on the tragedies that have plagued the Kennedy family, so eloquently responded, *"Adversity is only given to those who are willing to accept great responsibility."*

Looking back, it seems to me
All the grief that had to be
Left me when the pain was over
Stronger than I was before.
– Author Unknown

Failure doesn't mean that I'm a failure;

It does mean I have not yet succeeded.
Failure doesn't mean I have accomplished nothing,
It does mean I have learned something.

Failure doesn't mean I have been a fool,
It does mean I had enough faith to experiment.

Failure doesn't mean I have been disgraced,
It does mean I have dared to try.

Failure doesn't mean I don't have it,
It does mean I have something to do in a different way.

Failure doesn't mean I am inferior,
It does mean I am not perfect.

Failure doesn't mean I have wasted my life,
It does mean that I have an opportunity to start over.

Failure doesn't mean that I should give up;
It does mean that I should try harder.

Failure doesn't mean that I will never make it;
It does mean that I need more practice. Failure doesn't mean that I'm
a failure;
It does mean I have not yet succeeded.

Failure doesn't mean I have accomplished nothing,
It does mean I have learned something.

Failure doesn't mean I have been a fool,
It does mean I had enough faith to experiment.

Failure doesn't mean I have been disgraced,
It does mean I have dared to try.
Failure doesn't mean I don't have it,

It does mean I have something to do in a different way.

Failure doesn't mean I am inferior,
It does mean I am not perfect.

Failure doesn't mean I have wasted my life,
It does mean that I have an opportunity to start over.

Failure doesn't mean that I should give up;
It does mean that I should try harder.

Failure doesn't mean that I will never make it;
It does mean that I need more practice.
—Author Unknown

38

Certificate of Authenticity

"Most people were raised to believe they are just as good as the next person. I was told I was better." -Katharine Hepburn (1907 - 2003)

They broke the mold when they made me." It couldn't be more accurate. You are an original and not a copy. I heard a man once say, *"The greatest tragedy in life is being born an original and dying a carbon copy of someone else."* There are no two fingerprints alike. Therefore, no two people are alike. We are completely original works of art skillfully fashioned together. Don't try to be someone who you are not. Be true to yourself. The world is desperately searching for authenticity and despising counterfeits.

You are the right height, the perfect shape, and the ideal color. You have the greatest smile, the prettiest eyes, and the greatest personality. You are wonderful exactly the way you are because you have been *"fearfully and wonderfully made."*

There will always be things about ourselves that we would like to change, but don't make changing those things a lifelong quest. Change the things you can, accept and enjoy the things you can't—see them as your own stamp of uniqueness.

Teach your child that his/her own uniqueness and authenticity are the rarest of all treasures.

39

The Power of Integrity

"In all things showing yourself to be a pattern of good works; in doctrine showing integrity, reverence, incorruptibility...."
-The Bible - Titus 2:7 (NKJV)

"The integrity of the upright will guide them...."
- The Bible - Proverbs 11:3 (NKJV)

A person of integrity is solid, ethical, incorruptible and complete. People with integrity are committed to their own code of ethics. Their lives flow like a symphony of good works. They have nothing to hide and nothing to obscure. They say what they mean and mean what they say.

    A person of integrity consistently tries to do what is right even during difficult times. Integrity in its purest form is what you do when no one is watching. I recently heard someone say, "Reputation is what others think about you. Character is what you think about yourself."

Teach your child that integrity and character are more important than reputation.

40

Equity

"Loyalty to the principles upon which our government rests positively demands that the equality before the law which it guarantees to every citizen should be justly and in good faith conceded in all parts of the land." - Grover Cleveland (1837-1908)

Equity defined is, "The quality or state of being fair or just." God is a just God and requires nothing less from us. Always be fair in personal and business relationships. Our nation was built upon the ideas presented in the Declaration of Independence including one of the most famous lines in history, "*…that all men are created equal.*"

Different does not mean *less than* or *better than* another individual. Different just means *different* and nothing more. Fairness is giving people the treatment they deserve, which is what equality is all about. This topic of discussion is an excellent opportunity to teach your child about equity and fairness and to reaffirm the *Golden Rule*: "Do unto others as you would have them do unto you."

39

The Power of Integrity

"In all things showing yourself to be a pattern of good works; in doctrine showing integrity, reverence, incorruptibility...."
-The Bible - Titus 2:7 (NKJV)

"The integrity of the upright will guide them...."
- The Bible - Proverbs 11:3 (NKJV)

A person of integrity is solid, ethical, incorruptible and complete. People with integrity are committed to their own code of ethics. Their lives flow like a symphony of good works. They have nothing to hide and nothing to obscure. They say what they mean and mean what they say.

    A person of integrity consistently tries to do what is right even during difficult times. Integrity in its purest form is what you do when no one is watching. I recently heard someone say, "Reputation is what others think about you. Character is what you think about yourself."

Teach your child that integrity and character are more important than reputation.

40

Equity

"Loyalty to the principles upon which our government rests positively demands that the equality before the law which it guarantees to every citizen should be justly and in good faith conceded in all parts of the land." - Grover Cleveland (1837-1908)

Equity defined is, "The quality or state of being fair or just." God is a just God and requires nothing less from us. Always be fair in personal and business relationships. Our nation was built upon the ideas presented in the Declaration of Independence including one of the most famous lines in history, "*...that all men are created equal.*"

Different does not mean *less than* or *better than* another individual. Different just means *different* and nothing more. Fairness is giving people the treatment they deserve, which is what equality is all about. This topic of discussion is an excellent opportunity to teach your child about equity and fairness and to reaffirm the *Golden Rule*: "Do unto others as you would have them do unto you."

41

The Power of The Tongue

"There is one who speaks like the piercings of a sword, but the tongue of the wise promotes health." - The Bible - Proverbs 12:18 (NKJV)

"The tongue of the wise uses knowledge rightly, but the mouth of fools pours forth foolishness."- The Bible - Proverbs 15:2 (NKJV)

"Whoever guards his mouth and tongue keeps his soul from troubles." -The Bible - Proverbs 21:23 (NKJV)

The Bible has a lot to say about how we use the most creative power in the world—our mouths. Because we are created in the image and likeness of God, we have the same creative power that abides in Him, available to us. Everything God arranged, rearranged and spoke into existence, He did by His words. So, whether we realize it or not, our lives will be the very result of the words we speak.

God never breaks the laws and principles that He established in the arrangement of this world. The Bible says, "There will be spring time and harvest…" It also says, "There will be sowing and reaping and life *and* death." Another principle that God has set in order is, "You will have whatever you say…"

Teach your child these principles about the power of spoken words and that these principles were designed so that human beings can be the innovative creatures that God intended.

GEARED FOR GREATNESS

Affirmation #8

- I declare my child turns life's lemons into lemonade.

- I declare my child will always rise from the ashes of adversity.

- I declare my child is whole in spirit and operates in integrity.

- I declare my child treats everyone with dignity and respect.

- I declare my child learns to control what comes out of his/her mouth.

- I declare I have embraced every failure in my life and have used it as a stepping stone.

- I declare my child embraces his/her originality and authenticity.

- I declare I face adversity with courage and embrace the chance to learn something new about myself.

- I declare I treat everyone with dignity and respect.

- I declare I choose my words wisely.

Questions

What have I learned in the last few chapters?
(Failure and Adversity; Certificate of Authenticity; The Power of Integrity; Equity; The Power of The Tongue)

Where can I improve?

Do I consistently operate with integrity? If not, what areas in my life do I need to change?

What practices can I implement to control the words that come out of my mouth?

List ten negative things I need to stop saying:
1.
2.
3.
4.
5.
6.
7.
8.
9.
10.

42

Attitude

The longer I live, the more I realize the impact of attitude on life. Attitude to me is more important than facts. It is more important than the past, than education, than money, than circumstances, than failures, than successes, than what other people think or say or do. It is more important than appearance, giftedness or skill. It will make or break a company ...a church ...a home. The remarkable thing is we have a choice everyday regarding the attitude we will embrace for that day. We cannot change our past ...we cannot change the fact that people will act in a certain way. We cannot change the inevitable. The only thing we can do is play on the one string we have, and that is our attitude. I am convinced that life is 10% what happens to me and 90% how I react to it. And so, it is with you. We are in charge of our attitudes." - Charles Swindoll (1935-)

Teach your child that the choice of his/her attitude determines the outcome of his/her day.

43

Be Self-Motivated

Self-motivation is a discipline and strength that when implemented and practiced will place you in a small but powerful group of people. Not everyone can pull off this form of lifelong discipline. Self-motivated people have learned to reject mediocrity. They strive daily to scale the mountain of high achievement. They do not depend on other people for inspiration and they make the daily choice to arouse the giant within. I believe there are five traits that highly successful people possess.

They are fully engaged - Life is not passing them by. They remain present in the moment and maximize the opportunity of the hour.

They possess a sense of purpose - They are amazingly driven by the fact that the sky is the limit. They believe that there is nothing they cannot accomplish. They set goals and accomplish them.

Dressed for success - Success to them is something they "*are*" not something they are "*becoming*." It is impossible for them to fail. They *wear* their success.

Embrace adversity - They don't cower under the pressure of difficult situations. They use difficult situations as stepping stones into the world of greatness.

They are perpetual learners - They make learning a consistent discipline. They make it a point to perfect their craft.

Teach your child the act of positive reinforcement. Teach him/her the principle that his/her most dominant thoughts will determine the outcome of what he/she does. What your child does will determine who your child becomes. Who your child becomes will determine what your child achieves.

44

Boundaries Are Important

By definition, a boundary is, "Something that indicates or fixes a limit." One of the greatest concepts I have learned from life coach Dr. Phil McGraw is, *"You teach people how to treat you."* People generally believe they are victims of other people's behavior, rather than see that they are the victims of their own behavior.

Setting boundaries is the ability to know what you want out of life and then enforcing it. It is acknowledging you don't have to settle for anything less than what you deserve. It doesn't mean being picky. It just means not compromising values. Generally, people compromise to get something quickly, opting for instant gratification.

Teach your child not to accept less and be willing to wait for the best. Show your child by example what your boundaries are and teach your child how to set his/her own age-appropriate boundaries.

45

No Job Is Beneath You

The 39th President of the United States of America, Jimmy Carter, so eloquently stated, *"There is no difference between the greater and the lesser work."* According to one source, Jimmy Carter taught Sunday school for years at a Baptist Church in Plains, Georgia. He was both a President of a nation and a Sunday school teacher at church.

I have taught my children that the best workers are those who will do what it takes to get the job done. Teamwork is far more important than position and recognition. If one person wins, we all win.

Teach your child to participate in whatever needs to be done to get the job done.

46

Clean Up After Yourself

"Sometimes the greatest impression is the one you left behind."
- John Wooden (1910 - 2010)

If you mess it up, clean it up. This was our family motto. No one should have to clean up the mess you make. Granted, included in parenting is the daily drudgery of picking up behind our children. But you must be able to identify when your job ends and your child's chores begin.

I have heard many parents talk about their teenager's messy room! This has been a battle I choose to fight with teens because I believe that it teaches them organization, discipline, and how to effectively manage their time. By keeping a neat room, they don't waste time looking for things they should have put away in the first place. One of the lessons I believe it has taught my children is how to effectively manage a household. It is hopefully teaching them how to not be an undue burden on their future wives or husbands.

From the time my children were old enough to understand and effectively follow my instructions, especially during the school year, I would have them lay out everything the night before that they needed for the following day. That way our mornings would generally run smoothly. A small task the night before can set your child up for success the following morning. My friends and family were always amazed that my five children and I could be out of the house in one-hour flat!

A wise counselor once told me that a person's life is a direct reflection of the condition of their surroundings. Teach your child not depend on others to clean up after them.

Teach your child to ask the question before leaving a mess for someone else to clean up, "If not me, who?" Asking this question is a consistent reminder to take responsibility for themselves.

Affirmation #9

- I declare my child has a great attitude and outlook on life.

- I declare my child learns to love people based on principle and not emotion.

- I declare my child establishes healthy boundaries in relationships.

- I declare my child is willing to work hard and embraces every job opportunity.

- I declare my child is neat, organized, and tidy.

- I declare I am neat, organized, and tidy.

- I declare I have a great attitude and outlook on life.

- I declare I learn to love people based on principle and not emotion.

- I declare I am establishing or re-establishing healthy boundaries in my relationships.

Questions

What have I learned in the past few chapters?
(Attitude; Be Self-Motivated; Boundaries Are Important; No Job Is Beneath You; Clean Up After Yourself)

Where can I improve?

What can I do to improve my attitude?

What can I do to teach my child to operate in a spirit of love?

47

You Are Valuable

"Anyone who has never made a mistake has never tried anything new."-
Albert Einstein (1879-1955)

"The tragedy is that so many people look for self-confidence and self-respect everywhere except within themselves, and so they fail in their search."-
Nathaniel Branden (1930-)

"Let the world know you as you are, not as you think you should be, because sooner or later, if you are posing, you will forget the pose, and then, where are you?"- Fanny Brice (1891-1951)

"Never be bullied into silence. Never allow yourself to be made a victim. Accept no one's definition of your life; define yourself."
- Unknown

To pass this concept on to your child, it is vital that you must believe that *who you are* is *sufficient*. If you are being the best person you can be, society's assessment of you does not matter. Know that you are valuable and that your existence on the face of this planet matters. Believe that without your life, something in this world would be missing.

Teach your child the same concept.

48

Reaping and Sowing

One of the most powerful principles operating on earth is *"The Law of Reciprocity."* What you give comes back to you multiplied. It is important to understand that the things we want most *must first be given*. For example, if you want respect, give respect and carry yourself in a respectful manner. If you want love, be a loving person to others. If you want kindness, impart kindness to others.

The only one controlling the quality of life and the quantity of return is you. Teach your child that respect, love, and kindness are like seeds. If your child plants these *"seeds,"* he/she will reap a bountiful harvest. Likewise, if your child does not plant positive *"seeds,"* your child should not expect a positive and full return.

49

Choose Your Battles Wisely

"Any fool can criticize, complain, condemn and most fools do. Picking your battles is impressive and fighting them fairly is essential." - Dale Carnegie
(1888 - 1955)

Strategically choose battles that are worth the wounds. Some attacks come to distract you from the task at hand and others come to impede your forward progress. You have 1,440 minutes in a day to make life-changing choices. Each minute is like money in the bank. It's often been said, "Lose the battle—win the war." A great deal of our time is spent fighting battles that are fueled by revenge, rivalry, and personal gain.

Engage only in battles that will catapult you into your next dimension of success. As a society, we expend too much energy on things that bear no eternal consequence or even truly matter at the end of the day. Remember, even when the battle is too great for you, there is no battle that God cannot win.

Teach your child not to waste time on battles with little or no meaningful consequences.

50

The Gift of Laughter

"A merry heart does good, like medicine...."
- The Bible - Proverbs 17:22 (NKJV)

Laughter defined is, "The act of expressing mirth or joy." Scientific studies have concluded that laughing produces wonderful benefits, such as:

- Laughter lowers blood pressure.
- Laughter reduces stress.
- Laughter increases muscle flexibility.
- Laughter boosts the immune system.
- Laughter triggers the release of natural painkillers.
- Laughter produces a sense of well-being.

Just because life is serious, doesn't mean you must take it seriously all the time. Teach your child that laughter is as good as medicine.

Teach this by frequently laughing with your child.

51

One Person Can Change the World

Albert Einstein, Betsy Ross, Winston Churchill, Florence Nightingale, Osama Bin Laden, Martin Luther King Jr., Johann Sebastian Bach, Helen Keller, Bill Gates, Louis Braille, George Washington Carver, Adolph Hitler, Jesus, Genghis Kahn, Barry Gordy Jr., Thurgood Marshall, Ted Bundy (one of the world's most infamous serial killers), Harriet Tubman, Christopher Columbus, Ted Kaczynski (Unabomber), and Duke Ellington. The list could go on and on. The point is that each one of these individuals is known for changing the world in one way or another.

It is not whether you can change the world, but rather, *how* you change the world that matters. Teach your child that just like attitude, he/she has a choice each day of how to use his/her gifts and talents. Encourage your child to change the world positively and discuss the differences between the great names and dishonorable names listed above.

Affirmation #10

- I declare my child sees his/her own value.

- I declare my child understands the power of giving.

- I declare my child is learning to choose his/her battles wisely.

- I declare my child is learning the power of laughter and loves to laugh.

- I declare my child will change the world in a positive manner.

- I declare I see the value in myself and do everything I can to make my child feel valuable.

- I declare I give out what I want to receive.

- I declare I choose my battles wisely and do not spend too much time on things I cannot change.

- I declare I learn to laugh and not take everything so seriously all the time.

Questions

What have I learned from the last few chapters?
(You Are Valuable; The Principle of Reaping and Sowing; Choose Your Battles Wisely; The Gift of Laughter; One Person Can Change the World)

Where can I improve?

What can I do to make my child feel valuable?

What can I do to make myself feel valuable?

52

Read! Read! Read!

"Oh, the places you will go!"
-Theodor Seuss Geisel (Dr. Seuss 1904 - 1991)

"The world is a book, and those who do not travel read only one page." -Saint Augustine (Dates unknown)

"A library is a hospital for the mind."
-Anonymous

"That is a good book which is opened with expectation and closed in profit." - Amos Bronson Alcott (1799-1888)

One of the most exciting events in my childhood was when the Britannica Encyclopedia salesman came by our home. It was even more exciting when my mother purchased a set! I devoured the information buried between the hard covers.

Books are knowledge and knowledge is power. Teach your child to embrace, cherish, respect, and love books. I am an avid reader and am consistently adding to my literary collection. You can go everywhere and anywhere within the pages of a book.

The ability to learn and gain knowledge by reading books is limitless. Many people without formal education or degrees have *self-educated* through the discipline of reading. Teach your child there is no better way than reading to boost vocabulary, enhance personal understanding of the world, expand horizons, travel the world for free and increase capacity to retain information.

53

Choose Your Friends Wisely

"He who walks with wise men will be wise, but the companion of fools will be destroyed." -The Bible - Proverbs 13:20 (NKJV)

"As iron sharpens iron, so man sharpens the countenance of his friend." - The Bible - Proverbs 27:17 (NKJV)

"Do not be deceived: Evil company corrupts good habits." -The Bible - I Corinthians 15:33 (NKJV)

I have seared in the hearts of my children that wise men choose friends wisely. Teach your child to choose friends wisely and not just for the sake of popularity or peer acceptance. Your child is far too important to keep company with just anyone. Children are often discerning in this area and have a "gut feeling" about a person's character. Teach your child to not ignore "gut feelings." It is important to choose friends who encourage you to grow in a positive direction and enhance who you are as a person.

54

First Impressions

"Sometimes one creates a dynamic impression by saying something, and sometimes one creates as significant an impression by remaining silent."- Dalai Lama (1391)

Put your best foot forward! It only takes the first three seconds of meeting a person for the first time to make a general assessment and form a first impression. First impressions leave indelible prints in our minds and are not easily erased. This general assessment or first impression usually determines interest in furthering a relationship or not. There are no *do-overs* when it comes to a first impression. A dear friend of mine always says, *"You never get a second chance to make a first impression!"*

Some suggested ways to make a good first impression:

- Be well groomed.
- Keep eye contact.
- Be well prepared.
- Listen attentively.
- Be polite.
- For my sons, shake hands firmly.
- Approach every situation as if you have something to offer.
- Know that you have nothing to prove.
- Smile and look friendly.
- Follow directions.

Teach your child positive ways of making a good first impression.

55

Say Cheese!

Nothing can take the place of a beautiful smile! In my home, mornings and evenings include the same mantra and my children know these words by heart, "Did you brush and floss your teeth?" There is no excuse for poor oral hygiene. Make sure your child knows that taking care of his/her teeth is a priority. As a parent, I make sure I do my part in ensuring my children have healthy teeth. I take my children to the dentist every 6 months as recommended.

For younger children, some parents use helpful props such as egg timers by the bathroom sink to assist children in brushing a decent amount of time. I simply mandate that everyone with teeth in my house must brush and floss them! Teach your child that after his/her permanent teeth grow in, he/she must take care of them and maintain them so they will last a lifetime.

Some Healthy Tips

- Brush at least three times a day.
- Brush all your teeth with equal attention.
- Limit sweet and sticky snacks.
- Brush for at least three minutes.
- Floss after every meal.
- Rinse with mouthwash or peroxide.

56

Be an Optimist

"I believe that things turn out best for those that make the best of the way things turn out." - John Wooden (1910 - 2010)

Your outlook on life depends greatly on how you look at what you see. One of my favorite stories drives home the importance of optimism:

There were two old men who were both confined to hospital beds. One was a pessimist, the other an optimist. The optimist was placed by the window. In vivid expression, he would tell his friend wonderful stories each day of children laughing and playing outside. He would describe in detail the beautiful array of flowers that lined the streets and the excitement of the hustle and bustle of everyday life. One day, the optimist died and the pessimist was moved to the bed by the window. He was so excited to finally see for himself what he had only heard about from his friend for so long. When he finally looked out the window, all he saw was a brick wall.

Teach your child that no matter what the circumstance may look like, an optimistic outlook will create a more positive and hopeful environment towards effecting change.

Affirmation #11

- I declare my child chooses friends wisely.

- I declare my child understands the importance of first impressions.

- I declare my child maintains an optimistic outlook on life.

- I declare that I choose my friends wisely and I can identify unhealthy relationships in my life and my child's life.

- I declare I make sure my child brushes and flosses his/her teeth three times a day.

- I declare I maintain an optimistic attitude.

GEARED FOR GREATNESS

Questions

What have I learned in the last few chapters?
(Read! Read! Read! Choose Your Friends Wisely; First Impressions; Say Cheese!; Be An Optimist)

Where can I improve?

How can I help my child keep an optimistic outlook on life?

How can I assist my child in choosing friends wisely?

57

If at First You Don't Succeed…

"Always bear in mind that your own resolution to succeed is more important than any one thing." - Abraham Lincoln (1809-1865)

Abraham Lincoln was the 16th President of the United States. He has been acknowledged as one of the greatest leaders in American history. Look at how many times he failed before he became successful. The following is one version of his life and career:

Failed in business	1831
Defeated for Legislature	1832
Failed in business again	1833
Elected to Legislature	1834
Sweetheart died	1835
Nervous breakdown	1836
Defeated for Speaker	1838
Defeated for Elector	1840
Elected to Congress	1846
Defeated in Congress	1848
Defeated for Senate	1855
Defeated for V.P.	1856
Defeated for Senate	1859
Elected President	1860

Teach your child if at first if you don't succeed try, try again. Especially so if your child has a bend or passion towards accomplishing or obtaining something he/she deems important.

58

Choose Your Mentors Wisely

Mentor defined is, "Wise advisor, teacher or coach." The purpose of mentorship is to create quality people who will pass what they've learned onto the next generation. The greatest legacy you can leave behind is a well-built life. Mentors are like compasses that guide us along un-navigated terrain. It has been said, "If you don't know where you are going, you will follow anyone." I
    It is easier to travel a well-paved path than an unpaved road. Mentorship is the process of impartation whether face to face or by means of virtual reality, meaning: internet, television, DVDs, CDs and the many ways technology affords us to learn these days. Teach your child to glean from people who add value to our society.

I read a story of a man who was walking through a cemetery when he noticed an inscription on one of the tombstones that read:

As you are now, so once was I
As I am now, you are sure to be.
So, may I say, as now I lie,
Prepare yourself to follow me.

He took out a piece of chalk and beneath the inscription wrote this:

To follow you I'm not content,
Until I know which way you went.
- Unknown

59

Opportunities Are Created

"The opportunity of a lifetime must be seized in the lifetime of the opportunity."
-Linda Ravenhill (Dates unknown)

"The world is thine oyster which I with sword will open."
- Shakespeare (1564-1616)

"Opportunity is a haughty goddess who wastes no time with those who are unprepared." - George S. Clason (1874-1957)

Opportunity is defined as, "A good chance for advancement or progress." Personally, I don't wait on opportunities, I create them. I believe the world is yours for the taking. Life is whatever you make it! One of the key elements of creating opportunities is the ability to see the glass half full rather than half empty. Every problem, every setback, every failure is a mechanism and *"an opportunity"* for incredible change.

Seizing the opportunity is acting while things are still fresh in your mind and not letting them slip into the pile of *"things to do that never get done."* There are times and seasons in life when a window of opportunity is only open for a split second. You must take full advantage of that time. Some opportunities may never come again. My friend's father used to say, "Some trains only pass through a train station once in a lifetime. Know when to board."

Teach your child to be alert, be prepared and be ready to move swiftly when an opportunity presents itself.

60

Divine Contentment

"Contentment sweetens every condition."
- Thomas Watson (1620-1686)

I vowed long ago that whenever I found myself sad or disappointed I would never *stay* in a continuous state of unhappiness with my present conditions. There is much in life to complain about. Every day you are presented with the opportunity to be unhappy or happy. The choice is always yours. We must learn to be content with whatever state we find ourselves in at the present moment. No two moments will ever be alike and life is always changing. Don't confuse contentment with settling.

Many times, we miss the beauty of the journey when we only concentrate and focus on the result. If you are alive you can always do more, get more, and be more. Teach your child that success is gained through the strength and power of the journey along the way.

Teach your child to be content during all stages of the journey.

61

Don't Fear Death

"Because I have loved life, I shall have no sorrow to die."
- Amelia Burr (1878-1968)

"People living deeply have no fear of death." - Anais Nin (1903-1977)

"We are confident, I say, and willing rather to be absent from the body, and to be present with the Lord."
- The Bible 2 Corinthians 5:8 (KJV)

Do not fear death. Why fear the inevitable? Life does not end at the cessation of this earthly body. We are all going to spend our eternity somewhere. I once heard a man say, *"Heaven and Hell are not punishments or rewards for this life. They are just the results of the road we decided to walk down."* The Bible says, *"Enter through the narrow gate; for wide is the gate and spacious and broad is the way that leads away to destruction, and many are those who are entering through it. But the gate is narrow (contracted by pressure) and the way is straitened and compressed that leads away to life, and few are those who find it"* (Matt 7:13-14, Amplified)."

Death is our access to eternity, and it is something we will never escape. The beauty of death is, we close our eyes in this world and open our eyes in the next. It should be a joyous occasion. It signifies that our assignment in this world is complete. We must sow the seeds into the world that God the master farmer gave us.

When an individual fears death it is usually because they either do not have an assurance of where they'll be going, or because they never accomplished on earth what they thought they would accomplish and have a sense of *"running out of time."* You don't get a second chance at life. The remedy for not fearing death is maximizing life. Teach your child first and foremost to have a blessed assurance that heaven is real and not a place to fear when death arrives. Secondly, teach your child to live life to the fullest, and make good decisions so a life full of accomplishments is lived without the regret of *running out of time*.

Affirmation #12

- I declare my child is persistent and does not quit when life becomes difficult.

- I declare my child admires people who contribute positively to society.

- I declare my child seizes every good and positive opportunity.

- I declare my child lives a life of contentment.

- I declare my child learns to press through any fear of death and not stay or get stuck in fear mode.

- I declare I am persistent and keep trying even when circumstances are difficult.

- I declare I identify people who will be good mentors for my child.

- I declare I help my child seize opportunities which are beneficial for his/her life.

- I declare I find contentment in my life.

- I declare I am learning to press through any fear of death and not stay or get stuck in fear mode.

- I declare I am courageous and I do not allow any fear of death to paralyze me.

Questions

What have I learned in the last few chapters?
(If at First You Don't Succeed; Choose Your Mentors Wisely; Opportunities Are Created; Divine Contentment; Don't Fear Death)

Where can I improve?

What can I do to teach my child to be content?

What areas in my life, if any, do I need to address regarding fear of death?

62

Don't Worry

"God grant me the serenity to accept the things I cannot change. The courage to change the things I can and the wisdom to know one from the other."-
Reinhold Niebuhr (1892-1971)

Worrying about things that you cannot control is an act of futility. Life is full of many things far beyond our power to change. For instance, skin color, height, parents, family members or place of birth—the list could go on and on. So, considering this list, focus all your energy, thoughts, and goals on what you *can* control. Be the best YOU that *you* can be! Teach your child that worry has no value and does not bring about change. Teach your child the well-known Serenity Prayer by Reinhold Niebuhr, as well as how to identify things he/she can change and things he/she cannot change in life.

63

Only What You Do for Christ Will Last

I find this poem attributed to Abraham Lincoln to be more than adequate in summing up our earthly stay:

>*This crowd on earth*
>*They soon forget*
>*The heroes of the past.*
>*They cheer like mad*
>*Until you fall and that's how long you last.*

>*But God does not forget*
>*And in his Hall of Fame*
>*By just believing in His son*
>*Inscribed you'll find your name.*

>*I tell you, friends, I would*
>*Not trade my name however*
>*Small inscribed up there*
>*Beyond the stars*
>*In that celestial hall.*

>*For any famous name on earth*
>*Or glory that they share*
>*I'd rather be an unknown here*
>*And have my name inscribed up there.*

Teach your child that accomplishments on earth are not as significant as some would like to believe. Accolades, fame, and fortune can only be enjoyed on earth. More importantly, teach your child to care most about what God thinks because the truth is, it really does not matter much what others think of us. Only what you do for Christ will last.

64

Be Prepared

Remain in a state of constant readiness. Unexpected events are a way of life. As much as is possible prepare for change. Yes, we should always be prepared for unexpected events, such as natural disasters, accidents, etc. Yet, a sudden increase in finances, responsibility or business can also come about unexpectedly and bring along a whole new set of challenges. A marketing consultant once told me, "*Your production should always equal your marketing.*" Many people have gone out of business because they got *too much business too soon* and were not prepared in advance.

It is important that you can do the right thing at the right moment. You may never know when you will have to step up to the plate and be in charge. Many people have missed awesome opportunities because of ill-preparedness. Don't wait until the opportunity comes. Prepare long before an opportunity ever arrives.

A beautiful edifice is the result of much planning. Before a building can ever be constructed, it goes through a long process of architectural and financial planning. The actual construction of a building is the result of good preparation and planning. So, it is with the completion of your goals, plans, and productions as well.

Teach your child that success lies in being well-prepared.

65

Make Wise Choices

"For which of you, intending to build a tower, does not sit down first and count the cost ...." - The Bible - Luke 14:28 (NKJV)

Making hasty choices with little or no thought or making emotional choices rather than wise choices may result in regrettable and irreversible situations. It is crucial that your choices support what you say your priorities are.

There is a choice
You must make,
In everything you do,
And you must always
Keep in mind the choice
You make, makes you,
–Unknown

Teach your child the difference between a wise choice and a hasty choice and share examples of both types of choices.

66

Be Resilient

Resiliency defined is, "The ability to quickly recover in the face of adversity." It is one of the greatest attributes you can exemplify to your children.

It reminds me of a story I heard about a young man by the name of Thomas. Thomas was unable to keep a consistent job. He was fired from one of his jobs for sleeping and another for accidentally starting a fire. He was never formally educated. By the age of 22, he was completely destitute. Today, we know *"Thomas"* as Thomas Alva Edison, the inventor of the phonograph, the light bulb and motion pictures.

Teach your child that adversity doesn't mean you must quit. It just means you must change direction.

Affirmation #13

- I declare my child does not worry and has a heart filled with peace.

- I declare my child loves God with all his/her heart, mind, and soul.

- I declare my child makes wise choices in every facet of life.

- I declare my child is resilient and strong in spirit.

- I declare I do not worry about things that I cannot control.

- I declare I love God with all my heart, mind, and soul.

- I declare I make wise choices concerning my child.

- I declare God is giving me the strength to be resilient and strong in spirit.

GEARED FOR GREATNESS

Questions

What have I learned in the last few chapters?
(Don't Worry; Only What You Do for Christ Will Last; Be Prepared; Make Wise Choices; Be Resilient)

Where can I improve?

How can I teach my children to love God more?

What needs changing in my life to have a better relationship with God?

What things do I need to stop worrying about?

67

Don't Abuse Your Authority

"Most anyone can stand adversity, but to test a person's character put him in power." - Abraham Lincoln (1809-1865)

When you find yourself in a position of authority, understand that it is not your opportunity to control people but rather manage them. As an authority figure, one of your responsibilities is to lead and guide people into their destiny. Leading people takes character and calls for a realistic view of your own self-worth.

Leadership is never meant to exalt your own self-importance. Teach your child that being in a position of authority tests one's character and carries responsibilities beyond the obvious.

Teach your child to not abuse authority to advance selfish ambitions, but rather, respect his/her own position and opportunity to manage and lead others.

68

Practice What You Preach

The greatest example is doing what you teach others to do. How can you be an effective parent if you don't even follow your own advice? Unfortunately, children are more apt to follow what parents do rather than what parents *say*. Be mindful of the lifestyle you live around your children. Don't practice any behavior that you do not want them to emulate. It is not only what we do in the open that matters but in private as well. We seem to think if it is not seen, it will not have an impact on another person. That could not be further from the truth.

    Never require or expect from anyone else what you are unwilling to do yourself. In our humanness, we sometimes set standards for others, which we are unable to adhere to ourselves. To be a great person, you must lead by example. You can't preach what you don't know, and you can't lead where you won't go.

Teach your child not to just talk the talk, but to walk the walk he/she talks. Teach your child to live by high standards and not simply require high standards of others.

69

Love Never Fails

"Although I speak with the tongues of men and of angels, but have not love, I have become sounding brass or a clanging cymbal. And though I have the gift of prophecy, and understand all mysteries and all knowledge, and though I have all faith, so that I could remove mountains, but have not love, I am nothing. And though I bestow all my goods to feed the poor, and though I give my body to be burned, but have not love, it profits me nothing. Love suffers long and is kind; love does not envy; love does not parade itself, is not puffed up; does not behave rudely, does not seek its own, is not provoked, thinks no evil; does not rejoice in iniquity, but rejoices in the truth; bears all things, believes all things, hopes all things, endures all things. Love never fails... ...Pursue love..."
- The Bible - I Corinthians 13:1-8, 14:1 (NKJV)

Love is an abiding force that distinguishes us from all other living creatures in this world. Love is something we choose, not something we fall into, as in *falling in love*. I made the decision long ago that I would never leave this world without the people who meant the most to me knowing I loved them from the bottom of my heart.

Tell your family and friends often how much you love them. No one will ever know how you feel unless you express it through both words *and* actions. The cemetery is overflowing with people standing at tombstones wishing they had expressed their love for their now departed loved ones. They spend countless hours at the cemetery crying over the dead. My mother died when I was 19 years old and my grandparents died a few years later. Since their deaths, I have never felt the need to visit and take flowers to their graves because I gave them their flowers while they were alive. Teach your child that love is not only something you say but something you do.

Teach your child that falling in love is a myth and that he/she makes the choice to love someone.

70

You Cannot Fail If You Do Your Best

One year my oldest son was struggling in his math class and he asked me, "Mommy, is a 'C' a bad grade?" My response was, "No, not if you did your best." You can never fail if you give it your all. Grades don't always determine if you did your best or not. It is the honest effort that counts. Teach your child to do his/her best and to interpret failure accurately and not just by a grade.

At God's footstool to confess
A poor soul knelt and bowed his head
"I failed," he cried. The master said,
"Thou didst thy best that is success."
– Author Unknown

71

Work Hard

"No matter how much you want, laziness won't help a bit, but hard work will reward you with more than enough."
- The Bible - Proverbs 13:4 (CEV 1995)

Be diligent in everything that you do. Hard work is the product of an ambitious spirit. Embed in your child that hard work and giving 100% is a sign of excellence. No one can get anywhere without hard work. If you think you can, you are sadly mistaken. Overnight success doesn't happen overnight. When the media reports an "overnight success," they do our society a disservice, especially to young people who are so impressionable. One responsible American sportswriter Grantland Rice (1880-1954) wrote:

You wonder how they do it
You look to see the knack
You watch the foot in action
Or the shoulder or the back
But when you spot the answer
Where the higher glamours lurk,
You will find in moving higher
Up the laurel-covered spire
That most of it is practice
But the rest of it is work

Teach your child that hard work produces results and rewards! Teach your child there is no such thing as an "overnight success."

Affirmation #14

- I declare my child will never abuse authority as a future leader, boss, employer, teacher or parent.

- I declare my child lives by the same standards he/she requires of others.

- I declare my child learns the beauty of saying "I love you," and says it often.

- I declare my child is diligent in everything he/she does.

- I declare my child is not hindered or crippled by failure, but embraces it as an opportunity to learn something new.

- I declare that as a parent I do not abuse my authority. I do not use guilt or manipulation to discipline my child.

- I declare I do not require more of my child than I require of myself.

- I declare I can express love to my child verbally as well as demonstrate my love through hugs and affection.

- I declare I am not afraid of failure and embrace it as an opportunity to learn something I didn't know about myself.

Questions

What have I learned from the last few chapters?
(Don't Abuse Your Authority; Practice What You Preach; Love Never Fails; You Cannot Fail If You Do Your Best; Work Hard)

What can I do better?

What can I do to teach my child to be a good and effective leader?

How can I creatively show my child that I love him/her?

How well do I deal with failure? What can I do to deal with failure more positively?

What can I do to teach my child to deal with failure?

72

Know When to Help

Doing things for people when they can do it for themselves is not helping them at all. It is an impediment and cripples a person from becoming self-reliant. There is nothing wrong with helping people. But helping people to the point of creating helplessness is fruitless. Be a wise discerner when it comes to lending a helping hand. Often, people just dive in and begin "helping" when help was never requested. Wait to be asked for help and then make it your responsibility to enable people and not disable them by helping too much. Also, remember that doing too many things for too many people at one time leaves you drained and depleted.

Teach your child to be willing to help when help is requested and to be discerning when lending a helping hand.

73

Apology Accepted

You will never be able to keep relationships if you don't learn the art of apologizing. Apologizing is a difficult process and is only for the mature and responsible. Only responsible people are willing to accept fault and heal the breaches in relationships that conflict can bring. Failing to say, *"I am sorry"* when an apology is warranted leaves a feeling that things were never quite resolved. The inability to acknowledge fault leaves behind a trail of unresolved and broken emotions.

For several months, my relationship with my oldest son was severely strained. I could not quite pinpoint the problem. I finally concluded that the reason things felt unresolved was because he had not apologized and accepted responsibility for previous situations where he failed to follow instructions. I explained to him that failing to admit wrongdoing keeps you in a perpetual cycle of conflict. Generally, most people are willing to accept your apology if you are willing to admit fault.

Teach your child that apologizing is a sign of maturity and is a strength, not a weakness.

74

Replaceable You

It's a true statement that there is no one like you on this earth. We are all individuals uniquely created. However, never think that you are irreplaceable when it comes to a job or a position held. In these arenas, everyone is dispensable and everyone can be replaced. The show can *and will* go on without you. American Poet, Ogden Nash wrote:

Sometime when you are feeling important
Sometime when your ego's in bloom
Sometime when you take it for granted
You are the best qualified in the room

Sometime when you feel that you're going
Would leave an un-fillable hole
Just follow this simple instruction
And see how it humbles your soul

Take a bucket and fill it with water
Put your hand in it up to the wrist
Pull it out and the hole that's remaining
Is the measure of how you will be missed

You may splash all you please when you enter;
You can stir up the water galore
But stop and you will find in minutes
That it looks quite the same as before

The moral in this quaint example
Is to do just the best that you can,
Be proud of yourself, but remember
There is no indispensable man!

GEARED FOR GREATNESS

Teach your child everyone is replaceable when it comes to a job or a position. Teach your child there will always be both someone more qualified and someone less qualified in his/her midst, for as long as he/she lives.

75

Don't Take Shortcuts

"It takes more time to do something over than it takes to do it right the first time." - John Wooden (1910 - 2010)

Sometimes, the greatest life lessons are learned on a long road rather than a short path. People who cut corners never fully realize their God-given potential because they are always looking for an easy way out or a shortcut. Taking shortcuts is a sign of laziness and sometimes, it is a sign of arrogance. Remember the story of the tortoise and the hare? Teach your child to not get caught in the trap of taking shortcuts.

Teach your child to do a good job without shortcuts when taking on chores, tasks, jobs or assignments.

76

Don't Measure Success by Possessions

Some people measure a person's success by possessions owned, rather than by personal and professional accomplishments. The triumph of a person's life should be measured by what was given during a lifetime and not by what was amassed. It is hard *not* to pay attention these days, and be impressed by those who can afford luxury items and live elaborate lifestyles. As a society, we tend to give rich people, famous people, and celebrities far too much credit simply for being rich, famous or having celebrity status.

Yet, truly there are many people and unsung heroes who have accomplished great things in their daily lives who will never get an ounce of credit, recognition or even a mere mention. I've always said, "I would much rather be a private success and a public failure than a public success and a private failure." Genuine success is doing the best you can with what you've got to work with.

Teach your child that "things" are not the measurement of success.

77

Fearless!

"Always do what you are afraid to do."
- Ralph Waldo Emerson (1803-1882)

Fear is a powerful emotion. It can become a self-inflicted prison that keeps you from fulfilling your God-given purpose. It can totally and completely paralyze a person. Don't let fear dominate your life or you will never accomplish anything. Many times, the things we fear never even materialize.

The very nature of fear is to hinder your forward progress and upward mobility. It is okay to be afraid, but you **must** press through fear. Teach your child that being afraid is not the same as being fearful. Being afraid is a momentary reaction. Being full of fear is something that can linger for a lifetime if you refuse to overcome it.

Teach your child that F.E.A.R. is a good acronym to remember for conquering fear: False Evidence Appearing Real.

78

Respect Nature

One of God's greatest expressions of true beauty is seen in nature. We have been placed on this planet to be good stewards of nature and not to destroy it. Make it your personal mission in life to care for the world around you. We must make it our duty to leave the world better than we found it.

We have been graced with the pleasure of watching the sun dance across the morning sky, the privilege of viewing the majestic mountain ranges and the splendor of walking the beaches as the ocean ebbs and flows over our feet.

These are a few of my suggestions

- Recycle.
- Don't Litter.
- Don't destroy plants.
- Don't unnecessarily kill insects.
- Be an advocate for animals.
- Go green.

Teach your child that respecting nature is his/her responsibility.

Affirmation #15

- I declare my child is helpful but does not cripple people by helping them too much.

- I declare my child knows how to say "No," without feeling guilty.

- I declare my child does not cut corners or take shortcuts but does everything in excellence.

- I declare my child does not equate success with having possessions.

- I declare my child is not overcome by fear in any area of his/her life.

- I declare I am helpful, but I don't cripple people by helping them too much.

- I declare I know how to say "No" to people without feeling guilty, including my own child.

- I declare I exhibit a spirit of humility to my child.

- I declare I do everything in excellence.

- I declare my child understands that he/she has an important assignment on this earth and that he/she is not just taking up space.

- I declare I do not overwork myself and spend too little time with my child to obtain more possessions.

- I declare I understand I have an important assignment on this earth, and I am not just taking up space on earth or wasting time.

- I declare that every area in my life where I have been crippled by fear, I am being released from it right now.

- I declare my child appreciates the world we live in and respects nature.

Questions

What have I learned in the last few chapters?
(Know When to Help; Apology Accepted; Irreplaceable You; Don't Take Shortcuts; Don't Measure Success by Possessions; Fearless! Respect Nature)

What can I do better?

Who do I help too much and need to stop helping?

In what areas must I stop feeling guilty?

How can I better exercise a spirit of humility when interacting with my child?

List all the areas where you are afraid and release yourself from them by saying, "I break the power of fear over my life concerning _____."

GEARED FOR GREATNESS

How can I better teach my child to respect nature?

List all the areas where you know your child is fearful and release him/her by proxy by saying, "I break the power of fear over my child's life concerning_____:"

79

Obedience, The Ultimate Quality

"If you are willing and obedient, you shall eat the good of the land." -The Bible - Isaiah 1:19 (NKJV)

I once heard a story about a mother who told her son to stop jumping on the bed. He stopped jumping but he told his mother, *"I am still jumping on the bed on the inside."* Pure obedience is doing what you are told, when you are told and without internal resistance.

The strength of a human life depends on a sturdy foundation built on obedience. All of life is governed by rules and regulations and no one is exempt from the consequences of either following them or not following them. One well-known story and lesson in the perils of disobedience is the Biblical story about the children of Israel wandering in the wilderness for over 40 years—a journey that should have taken them only a few days had they been obedient and without complaint.

Teach your child that obedience is a noble quality and it will assist him/her in leading a fruitful and productive life.

80

The Green-Eyed Monster

"For jealousy is the rage of a man: therefore, he will not spare in the day of vengeance." - The Bible - Proverbs 6:34 (NKJV)

Jealousy defined is, "The act of being resentfully suspicious of rivalry." Jealously is a destructive, angry, and devastating emotion. It is a very difficult emotion to overcome and is a constant challenge for the person who struggles with it. In my experience, I have found that many people who struggle with jealousy are plagued with feelings of envy, confusion, insecurity, and worthlessness. These feelings are often at the root of abusive relationships that result in physical violence.

If not nipped in the bud and controlled, jealousy will only continue to grow and escalate. I especially teach my daughters to stay clear of anyone who exhibits any type of jealous behavior. There is nothing healthy about being jealous of someone or someone being jealous of your child. Teach your child that possessiveness and jealousy are not signs of love and to steer clear of jealous individuals.

Teach your child to recognize the tactics of jealousy. The following is what experts say:

Tactics used by jealous individuals:

o   Making all the decisions in a relationship.
o   Monitoring whereabouts.
o   Monitoring relationships with friends or family.
o   Name calling.
o   Threatening violence.
o   Using anger and control to manipulate.

Ways to deal with anger and jealousy

- Look at how your own behavior has affected past relationships.
- Focus on reality, not perception.
- Realize your mate chose you for a reason and found something special in you.
- Get counseling.
- Establish guidelines for your relationship early on and enforce them.

81

Be A Motivator

Life can be extremely difficult. Everyone at some point in life needs someone to help them through rough times and coach them to the finish line. Be a motivator and an encourager. Be the one standing on the sidelines cheering others saying, "You can make it!" In doing so, it is highly likely that when you need a little push, there will be someone there to cheer you on as well! We reap what we sow. Fortunately, this means the good stuff too!

Teach your child that only the courageous have the power to encourage and motivate others.

82

The Dangers of Greed

"Money is like manure, it needs to be spread around or it begins to stink." - J. Paul Getty (1892-1976)

"Hell and destruction are never full; so, the eyes of man are never satisfied." - The Bible - Proverbs 27:20 (NKJV)

Greed defined is, "A selfish desire to obtain money, wealth, material possessions or more than a person legitimately needs, usually at the expense of others." The Bible refers to greed as the sin of covetousness and it is listed as one of the seven deadly sins. The essence of greed is having a desire for more than you are morally entitled to.

The prison system is bursting with individuals who were driven by the demon known as greed. These individuals did anything and used anyone to get what they wanted.

Teach your child the only thing that cures the greedy soul is a generous spirit.

83

Wealth or Prosperity?

Wealth defined is, "The abundance of material possessions or resources." Prosperity, on the other hand, is defined as, "The enjoyment of a vigorous, healthy and vital life." People place so much emphasis on acquiring material possessions that they lose sight of the true riches in life—love, family, peace, and hope. Warren Buffet the second richest man in the world has his priorities straight. He gave away 31 million dollars to charity.

I would much rather be comfortable and enjoy great peace with my family than to have great wealth and be alone. The blessings of the wealthy are momentary and like the adage says, "You can't take it with you." Yet, true prosperity can last a lifetime. It is very possible to be wealthy and not have prosperity or to have prosperity and not be wealthy. Our society consistently confirms the fact that wealth does not bring you peace. I received an e-mail some time ago concerning our love affair with money. These are the valuable words I read in that e-mail:

> *"You can buy a house, but you cannot buy a home;*
> *You can buy a bed, but you cannot buy sleep;*
> *You can buy a clock, but you can't buy time;*
> *You can buy a book, but you can't buy knowledge;*
> *It can earn you a position but not respect;*
> *It can buy you medicine, but it can't buy you health;*
> *It can buy you blood, but it can't buy you life."*
> *Nothing in life worth having can be paid for.*

The real measure of a man's wealth is how much he'd be worth if he lost all his money." - Anonymous

Teach your child the wealthy are not always prosperous but the prosperous are always rich in spirit.

Affirmation #16

- I declare my child has an obedient spirit and does not give in to a spirit of rebellion.

- I declare my child is not jealous but feels secure and important not based on another person's security and importance.

- I declare my child is quick to motivate and support the efforts of others.

- I declare my child is generous and not greedy.

- I declare my child understands that prosperity is more optimal than wealth and that prosperity is more valuable than money.

- I declare I am courageous and consistent in disciplining my child when he/she is disobedient.

- I declare I don't confuse jealousy with love.

- I declare I am quick to motivate and support the efforts of others.

- I declare I am not greedy but instead generous with my resources and time.

- I understand prosperity is more valuable than money and far more important than earthly wealth.

Questions

What have I learned in the last few chapters?
(Obedience, The Ultimate Quality; The Green-Eyed Monster; Be A Motivator; The Dangers of Greed; Wealth or Prosperity?)

What can I do better?

What can I do to reward my child's obedience?

If I am in a relationship involving jealousy by either myself or my partner, am I willing to get help and break the cycle for the sake of my child?

What can I do to better motivate my child?

Am I doing anything that perpetuates sibling rivalry in my household? If so, what steps can I take to stop it?

What can I do to make my child feel special and important?

84

Pride, Arrogance, And Confidence - The Distinction

"Let nothing be done through selfish ambition or conceit, but in lowliness of mind let each esteem others better than himself."
- The Bible - Philippians 2:3 (NKJV)

The spirit of pride wages a brutal war on the humble soul. Humility is one of the few human characteristics that can determine our providence. When you know you are great at something, you don't have to spend all your time convincing other people that you are great. People will discover your greatness on their own. Pride is a destructive force that eventually puts you in the pits of life. A prideful spirit is un-teachable, unforgiving, and stubborn. No one wants to be around a prideful person. As the adage says, *"One bad apple spoils the whole barrel."* You can rest assured a prideful person will soon be taking a fall of some sort. Recognizing prideful behavior and shaking it off before it takes root is a significant discovery.

Arrogance on the other hand is defined as an, "Exaggeration of one's own worth or importance in an overbearing manner." Arrogance is most often insecurity in reverse. It is a feeble attempt to establish significance and value. Everyone is searching for significance. Many people who suffer from arrogance spend a lifetime trying to establish value and a sense of self-worth and any hint of disapproval sends them spiraling downward into an abyss of depression. Teach your child true value is found from within and is not a result of what people think of you.

There is a fine line between confidence and arrogance, and it is very easy to get the two confused. The confident believe in their abilities but also have learned how to embrace constructive criticism. The arrogant on the other hand reject any form of criticism and correction. It is imperative that you learn to receive constructive criticism as a catalyst for personal growth. I learned a long time ago that you are never as good as you think and never as bad as they say. Nevertheless, self-inspection is warranted.

Teach your child the disadvantages of being prideful and arrogant and the rewards of self-confidence.

85

Keep Your Word

There is a vast chasm between promise and fulfillment. These days, taking people at their word is a difficult task. Too many people never deliver what they say they will. I teach my children the wise-saying, *"A man's word is his bond."* The success of relationships is directly impacted by the ability to make and keep promises. Keeping your word generates success in every area of your life. Your reputation is either based on consistency or inconsistency.

I remember years ago, a dear friend of mine said to me, *"You never keep your word."* This really struck a chord in my heart. I realized how easily I made obligations knowing I might be unable to fulfill them. Since that time, I have put forth every effort to keep my word when I commit to doing something for someone. It takes practice. In doing so, I have also learned to only make those commitments which are feasible and not simply things I *"desire"* to fulfill.

Teach your child to keep his/her word.

86

The Golden Rule

You shall love your neighbor as yourself..."
- The Bible Leviticus 19:20 (NKJV)

"Love has nothing to do with what you are expecting to get, it's what you are expected to give - which is everything." - Unknown

Do unto others the way you would have them do unto you. Treating people how you want to be treated is a universal law that has been found in the writings of almost every world religion known to man. It has been termed as the "ethic of reciprocity." It is giving every human being the respect due them. It is the basis of what Martin Luther King Jr. gave his life for—*Human Rights*. Every individual has the right to the principles established and written in the Declaration of Independence—Life, Liberty and the pursuit of Happiness... The Golden Rule is fueled by self-love, for you can never love anyone more than you love yourself.

Teach your child to treat people the way he/she, in turn, wants to be treated by others.

87

Choose Joy

"...The joy of the Lord is my strength."
- The Bible - Nehemiah 8:10 (NKJV)

Happiness is a state of mind that can easily be altered. Joy, if truly understood, is perpetual. Happiness is dependent on external activity whereas joy, on the other hand, comes from deep within and has nothing to do with external factors. Physical and emotional surroundings may not always include a happy set of circumstances. However, the force of joy from within can sustain the human spirit even in the bleakest of times. It is that force of joy alone that can be the difference between courage and defeat, strength, and weakness, peace and unrest, confusion or clarity. Joy can hold you together when everything around you is falling apart.

Teach your child the difference between happiness and joy. Choose joy!

88

Drinking, Driving and Drugs

The statistics for vehicular manslaughter because of drunk driving, among teens, is staggering. Sadly, it is on the rise. Driving is a responsibility, not a recreation. According to SADD (Students Against Destructive Decisions) 60% of all teenage deaths are related to drug and alcohol abuse.

It is a fact, many young people today engage in illicit, unlawful drug and alcohol use to alleviate the pain of unresolved emotions and to fit in with the *crowd*. Life is too valuable to treat as an experiment and too precious to speed up the process of death through the unlawful use of drugs and alcohol combined with driving a vehicle.

When a person knows, believes, and understands their purpose, as a valuable human being on earth, time and resources will not be wasted on things that can prematurely invite death. Obviously, this includes driving under the influence of any controlled or uncontrolled substance. Teach your child not to use drugs or drinking and driving as a recreational activity or to numb the pain of life. Teach your child that driving is a responsibility and drugs/alcohol are destructive.

I encourage you to visit and get your child involved with the SADD organization at www.sadd.org

Affirmation #17

- I declare my child is not arrogant or haughty.

- I declare my child is consistent in keeping his/her word and does not make promises he/she cannot keep.

- I declare my child is filled with joy from within every day of his/her life.

- I declare my child is not prideful but understands the power of humility.

- I declare my child is not or will not be addicted to drugs, alcohol, or any other harmful substance.

- I declare my child is kind, generous, and loves his/her neighbor as he/she loves himself/herself.

- I declare my child is a responsible driver and understands driving is a responsibility and not a recreational activity.

- I declare I do not think more highly of myself than I should, and I am willing and able to put other's needs before my own.

- I declare I keep my word, and I am consistent in doing what I say I am going to do.

- I declare I love my neighbor as myself and if I don't love myself, I declare everything preventing me from loving myself is being healed immediately.

- I declare the joy of the Lord is always my strength, and I don't rely on outward circumstances to dictate how I feel.

GEARED FOR GREATNESS

- I declare I am not addicted to drugs, alcohol, or any other harmful substance. If I do suffer from any of these addictions, I declare I will get help to, in turn, help my child be better geared for greatness.

- I declare I am a responsible driver and I am an example to my child.

Questions

What have I learned from the last few chapters?
(Pride, Arrogance, and Confidence—The Distinction; Keep Your Word; The Golden Rule; Choose Joy; Drinking, Driving, & Drugs)

What can I do better?

In what areas have I failed to keep my word?

What circumstances are causing me to lose my joy?

Stop focusing on the negative, List 10 things that you are grateful for and have your child do the same exercise below:
1.
2.
3.
4.
5.
6.
7.
8.

9.
10.

My child is grateful for:
1.
2.
3.
4.
5.
6.
7.
8.
9.
10.

89

To Know Thyself

One of the most crucial defenses you have in life is getting to know yourself. Learn what makes you tick. Learn what you like and don't like about yourself including your strengths and your weaknesses. If you learn this, it will be easier for you to navigate through the pitfalls of life and relationships. You will not accept things that you know you are not capable of handling. If you know yourself then you don't need anyone else to define you or tell you who you are.

The most incredible voyage you will ever take in life is inside your own heart, soul, and spirit. Your life's journey will be like following a treasure map, looking for hidden treasures. In the depths of your spirit, like sunken treasure in the bottom of the ocean, you will find pearls of wisdom and priceless rubies. Understanding yourself gives you the ability to better understand your fellow human being. Truly knowing yourself is understanding why you do what you do. If you never understand your motives, how will you ever effect change in your life?

Teach your child that his/her greatest possession is the hidden treasures of the heart.

90

Guard Your Heart

"Carefully guard your thoughts because they are the source of true life." - The Bible - Proverbs 4:23 (CEV 1995)

"For as he thinketh in his heart, so is he..."
- The Bible - Proverbs 23:7 (KJV)

We are responsible for our children—body, soul, and spirit. Be careful about what you allow your child to listen to or watch. Your eyes and ears are portals to your soul. Everything in my house is monitored including Internet, IPODs, television, video games, and the radio. Be mindful about what you allow to interfere with the atmosphere of your home and your child's spirit. What you see and hear affect your thoughts. Your thoughts affect the condition of your heart. The condition of your heart determines your actions. Your actions dictate your future. Your future decides your destiny.

    This next example may seem a bit extreme or graphic, but I believe that being extreme drives home the seriousness of this matter. One of the most notorious serial killers in America, Ted Bundy, spoke in an interview prior to his execution. One of the things he really stressed during the interview was the danger of pornography both audio and visual. He said that pornography had been the catalyst to his sadistic criminal, murderous behavior and patterns.

Teach your child the importance of protecting what goes in his/her ears and eyes.

91

Dreams Do Come True

"Some dream about becoming successful but others get up every day and work hard at it."- Unknown

"Dreams don't die, people do."
- Yvonne Denise Camper (1964 -)

Dream big or don't dream at all. Dreaming big requires that you eat, sleep, and drink what you desire. It requires incredible fortitude to make your dream happen. You become what you say, and you accomplish what you visualize. There is nothing that you cannot achieve if you put your mind to it. Be persistent and work hard. Do not be afraid to be innovative and different. Don't take no for an answer. Find another way if you run into roadblocks. The law of averages is on your side. If you fish long enough, eventually you are going to catch fish. Set realistic and reachable goals. I found a wonderful tool I use in my own project management and planning that assists me in setting viable goals, the acronym SMART. Goals should be:

S—specific, significant, stretching
M—measurable, meaningful, motivational
A—agreed upon, attainable, achievable, acceptable, action-oriented
R—realistic, relevant, reasonable, rewarding, results-oriented
T—time-based, timely, tangible, trackable

Teach your child that dreams are gifts to the soul and that dreams DO come true coupled with hard work and persistence.

92

Manage Your Health

"An ounce of prevention is worth a pound of cure."
- Benjamin Franklin (1706-1790)

People never miss their good health until they don't have it anymore. You only get one body—so use it wisely. Stop diseases before they start. How, you ask? Scientific studies and research have confirmed that eating right, exercising, and getting adequate rest are the best safeguards against a feeble body. Taking care of your body can sometimes be as easy as getting out and walking. The following are tips I recommend towards managing your family's health:

1. Nurture your inner person as well as your outer person. Design ways to daily release stress and tension out of your life.
2. Read your owner's manual daily (The Bible).
3. Create daily regimens to take care of your skin, hair and nails.
4. Drink plenty of water. It keeps the body fully hydrated, transports oxygen to the blood and helps carry nutrients throughout your system.
5. Go to the doctor. Many people unnecessarily suffer health conditions because they are either afraid of going to the doctor or don't find the value in it. If you can go to the physician on a regular basis, do so. I make it a point to stay current on my health regimens such as physicals, mammograms, and pap smears as well as staying current with my children's doctor appointments. Some health problems might be circumvented by just taking a more prevention-oriented and participatory stance in your own

healthcare.
6. Model these practices for your child. One day he/she will most likely model them for his/her children as well.

93

Stay Educated

"Do not train children to learn by force and harshness, but direct them to it by what amuses their minds, so that you may be better able to discover with accuracy the peculiar bent of the genius of each."
- Plato (429-347 B.C.E.)

"Education is not the filling of a bucket, but the lighting of a fire."
- William Butler Yeats (1865-1939)

Education is a lifelong process. We must consistently stay in the position of being inquisitive. With the utmost intention, continue to fan the flames of curiosity. Higher education takes consistency, dedication, discipline, courage, and self-motivation. Every year, I contact my children's teachers to let them know that I am fully engaged in my children's education. I consistently stress the importance of education to my children, whether vocationally or academically.

Not everyone is designed for college. Pay close attention and discern if college is for your child or not. If your child desires to go to college, never let the cost of an education make that decision. For some children, higher education does not always mean enrolling in college or in a secondary educational institution. Remember Bill Gates was a college drop-out. Teach your child to follow his/her heart and natural bent by seeking education that will lead him/her to his/her goals in life.

Teach your child that not all education is found in college and there are many choices when it comes to education and learning.

Affirmation #18

- I declare my child is true to his/her own nature and does not allow peer pressure to change him/her.

- I declare my child loves himself/herself and is content with how God made him/her.

- I declare my child can change the things about himself/herself that he/she does not like.

- I declare my child is not afraid to follow his/her dreams.

- I declare my child takes good care of his/her body and is not given to obesity.

- I declare my child drinks enough water to keep his/her body operating at its best.

- I declare I am true to my authentic self and do not allow people or circumstances to change who I am.

- I declare I love myself just the way I am and the things that need changing, I have the power and discipline to change.

- I declare I am not afraid to follow my dreams and know in my heart that it is never too late.

- I declare I take good care of my body.

- I declare I will do everything I need to achieve maximum health.

GEARED FOR GREATNESS

Questions

What have I learned in the last few chapters?
(To Know Thyself; Guard Your Heart; Dreams Do Come True; Manage Your Health; Stay Educated)

What can I do better?

What can I do to be true to my authentic self?

How can I teach my child to be true to his/her authentic self?

What do I love about myself that I would never change?

What can I do to teach my child to love himself/herself?

What dream have I been afraid to dream and what am I willing to do to make it become a reality?

What habits do I need to change so that I can improve my health?

How can I better improve my child's health?

94

Patience Is a Virtue

"Better is the patient spirit than the lofty spirit. Do not in spirit become quickly discontented, for discontent lodges in the bosom of a fool."
- The Bible - Ecclesiastes 7:8-9 (NAB)

"One moment of patience may ward off great disaster. One moment of impatience may ruin a whole life." - Chinese Proverb

"Patience and perseverance have a magical effect before which difficulties disappear and obstacles vanish."
- John Quincy Adams (1825-1829).

The greatest of all virtues is patience. Patience is the ability to endure waiting, delay, or provocation without becoming annoyed or upset. Patience is the ability to persevere calmly when faced with difficulties. Impatience, on the other hand, is the need for instant gratification. Sometimes we move too quickly. We have not learned the discipline of endurance. Waiting sometimes is viewed as a weakness, not an asset, but it should be considered as a strength.

Situations must be fully evaluated before you can make a viable decision. Waiting does not always mean that you are not ready. It may mean that the people who are necessary to assist you are not ready! Moving too swiftly can be quite costly and determine the difference between success and failure.

Teach your child that patience and perseverance are two very important disciplines that will greatly preserve his/her life.

95

Money and Credit Smarts

"It is more rewarding to watch money change the world than watch it accumulate."- Gloria Steinem (1934–)

"Money won't create success, the freedom to make it will."
- Nelson Mandela (1913–2013)

There are many ways to teach your children how to save money. Experts suggest:

1. Don't spend everything you earn.

2. Don't live beyond your means. If you can't afford it you just can't afford it.

3. Save at least 10% of your salary. It is an attainable goal. It is important that your child establishes a consistent habit of saving his/her money.

4. Account for your money. People who can account for their money spend far less and save more. Learn to balance your checkbook to the penny.

5. Save for a rainy day. You just never know when a rainy day will show up, but when it does, you will be prepared.

6. Credit cards are not money. Pay cash for everything. Keep credit cards for emergencies. If you are going to buy on credit pay the full amount on receipt of the monthly statement to avoid interest charges.

GEARED FOR GREATNESS

7. Give 10% of your income to your church or a charity of your choice.

96

Finish Strong

Finishing strong means not quitting. Not quitting even when every ounce of strength has been depleted from you emotionally, spiritually, and physically. Train yourself to go the distance. In life, you soon discover you will not always be on the winning team. Life may not be going quite as you planned now but make up your mind that quitting is never an option. The race is not always given to the swift nor the battle to the strong. Be like the runner who breaks the tape at the finish line after the influx of a second wind. It is so easy to quit when things are not turning out the way you had hoped. Strength comes in running the last lap.

Teach your child to leave a trail of excellence behind as he/she runs the race and to finish strong!

97

The Power of Prayer

"The effective, fervent prayer of a righteous man avails much."
- The Bible - James 5:16 (NKJV)

Understanding that *God is a refuge* in the face of daily pressures *is* the power found in prayer. Prayer is one of the greatest hidden secrets. It is the privilege we are afforded to talk to God about anything at any time! The Bible, Isaiah 26:3-4 (NKJV), states, *"You will keep him in perfect peace whose mind is stayed on you, because he trusts in you. Trust in the Lord forever..."* If you keep your mind on Him and trust Him for everything and in every situation, a perfected peace will embrace you. There is nothing too small and nothing so big that He can't understand. Learning the power of prayer relieves us from carrying unnecessary burdens. Christ said, *"My yoke is easy and my burdens are light..."* (Matthew 11:30, NKJV).

    It has been medically and scientifically proven that prayer works and has a positive impact on our lives. Prayer is a powerful force that closes the chasm between heaven and earth. By praying, we admit we don't have all the answers and that we have the courage to seek a power greater than our own.

Teach your child that God wants to hear everything he/she has to say!

98

Rejection and Criticism

Rejection is inevitable and it will happen to you like it happens to everyone else at one time or another. The word "no" will be uttered in your life more than you will ever care to hear it. Not everyone will believe in you or your hopes and dreams. The only thing that matters is that YOU believe in you, your hopes and your dreams. You alone hold the master blueprint to your dreams and ambitions.

Criticism is also inevitable. Not all criticism is bad or unwarranted. There is such a thing as constructive criticism. This is the valuable information shared with us by perhaps mentors, bosses, spouses, friends, and the people who are generally in our corner. Although it is human nature to not want to hear criticism, do allow constructive criticism to be shared with you. One of my best friends loves to remind me that four eyes are better than two and six eyes are better than four, meaning we all need the insight of others to reach our goals.

When it comes to rejection and criticism, the quest for you is to keep your eyes on what you envision. Don't turn away from it. It's what you know for sure, not what others say that will propel you into your future destiny. Someone once said, *"If you have no confidence in yourself, then you are twice defeated in the race of life. With confidence, you have won before you have started."*

Teach your child to recognize the differences between rejection and criticism and to welcome constructive criticism when offered by people who have his/her best interest at heart.

99

Lessons in Dating

Dating is not an experiment. Society says that you should date so you will know what you want and don't want in a mate. If you get to know yourself, you won't need anyone else's opinion to help you decide what makes you happy. A few of my suggestions are:

- o Don't repeatedly date anyone you've determined you would not be willing to marry. It is pointless to date someone who you would not even consider spending the rest of your life with and is merely a waste of your time and his/her time as well.

- o Don't date someone who doesn't have similar goals and aspirations because he/she will eventually become dead weight.

- o Don't date anyone who can't support the weight of your dreams.

- o Don't date anyone who does not have a good relationship with his/her family.

- o Don't date anyone who does not have a job or established goals.

Teach your child to be both cautious and deliberate when dating and make sure to go over dating rules and expectations as he/she enters different stages of life—mid-teens, later teens, young adult and even adult. When you've geared a child for greatness you can expect that the conversations of life's important issues will go on forever and that you will be viewed as a source of perpetual wisdom in your child's life.

100

Social Media and Texting: Blessing or Curse?

When I first wrote this book seven years ago, social media and texting, as we know it today, had not yet fully manifested. Although every technological advance can be used for the greater good, in the hands of the wrong person, it can morph into an untamed monster that is difficult to harness. I do believe positive things can come out of these forms of communication, but I am going to focus more on the negative aspect as this book is about teaching our children how to lead effective lives.

My children, who are now adults, are the by-products of the social media and texting revolution. Recently, they were expressing how difficult it is for them to focus and even sit down and read a book. One survey says that when people are unable to access their electronic devices, their anxiety levels go up - FOMO (fear of missing out) at its best.

Also, the texting craze has given rise to sexting, avoidance of conflict, and empty communication. It has diminished the amount of face-to-face and intimate conversations people have while at the same time reducing the quality of the human connection. I believe the long-term negative effects of social media and electronic communication have yet to be fully discovered.

The age of social media has given rise to countless teenage tragedies that have been horrific and heartbreaking. Unfortunately, social media platforms are also being used to fuel the "movie star" image and people's lust for fame. These days, how many "likes" you get is far more important than being a viable individual. The term "like" to this generation embodies the essence of social acceptance to the extent that ignoring one's online quest for approval creates social alienation.

We find today's child desperately craves the validation of people they don't even know. This method of acceptance is taking over the way people interact through social media. I believe this phenomenon has also given rise to more vicious and effective online bullying tactics. Knowing that with the touch of a button and the stroke of a key, a person's life can be destroyed in a split second is a scary thought.

Because keeping your child away from social media is so difficult, and there are now more cell phones on the planet than there are people, I feel as parents the children's social media activity must be heavily, and I emphasize heavily, monitored. Evaluating the maturity level of your child is also important because some children are just not at the level of maturity to even handle the vast amount of information that is being released. Specifically, I believe that children should not have access to social media platforms before the age of 10, and access should be minimal until age 13.

Also, from a parent's perspective, I find my anxiety level regarding the safety of my children is far higher than what my parents experienced when I was growing up. Our parents generally had no contact with us during day. It seems the more access my children, the more I have struggled with fear if they don't answer their phone or text me back. Our reliance on social media and texting has reduced our trust in God.

At this point, I find it more beneficial to focus on what I believe social media and texting are and what they are not.

Social media and texting are:

- A wonderful way to keep in contact with people and strengthen family bonds.
- A great mechanism to do research and access information.
- An effective way to promote and engage people in your social engagements.
- An efficient tool for communication when face-to-face meetings are not feasible.

Social media and texting are not:
- An avenue to air your dirty laundry and every detail about your life.

- A healthy way to boost and build your self-esteem.
- A substitute for real face-to-face communication and intimacy.
- A mechanism for "hooking" up or dating.
- A means to destroy or demean other people.

Teach your child that social media and texting are not the only means to communicate and that his or her value and self-worth is not contingent on these platforms. Also, take the time to explore different avenues of communication with your child.

Affirmation #19

- I declare my child gets enough rest and he/she is not hyperactive.

- I declare my child learns the value of saving money.

- I declare my child is given to prayer and seeking God for answers.

- I declare my child will take rejection and criticism gracefully.

- I declare my child is healed, right now, from the pain of rejection and criticism.

- I declare my child knows the difference between constructive criticism and mean-spirited criticism.

- I declare my child does not date until he/she is emotionally ready.

- I declare my child is proud of the parent who I am becoming.

- I declare I do not overload myself and always make time for refreshing my spirit.

- I declare I am learning to be more frugal with my money, and I appreciate the value of saving.

- I declare I am healed from the pain of rejection and criticism and know rejection and criticism do not define who I am.

- I declare that as I teach my child to be responsible on social media, I am modeling the same behavior.

- I make a vow to guard my child's heart and spirit by monitoring their social media and texting communication.

Questions

What have I learned in the last few chapters?
(Patience is a Virtue; Money Smarts; Finish Strong; The Power Of Prayer; Rejection And Criticism; Lessons In Dating; Parents, Social Media and Texting; Blessing or Curse?)

What can I do better?

What can I do to ensure that my child and I get an adequate amount of rest?

What can I do to spend more time in prayer and seeking God for my life and my child's life?

What areas of my life have I felt rejection and how have I let people's criticism define me?

What safeguards will you put in place to protect your child from negative social media interactions?

101

Your Child's 30-day Emotional Makeover

"We are so busy making a living that we forget to make a life." – John Wooden

Your child's 30-day emotional makeover is designed to not only strengthen your child, but strengthen your family as well. One source reports that most parents spend less than 30 quality minutes a day with their child. This lack of intimate connection can be detrimental to their self-worth and overall emotional well-being because children equate love with time. When we fail to spend a healthy amount of time with our children, feelings of rejection and abandonment can take root and negatively affect all their adult relationships.

These issues compounded with the expectations of academic achievement, peer pressure, and poor self-image can slowly chip away at their self-esteem. We believe that one of the bedrocks of success is a realistic self-image. When children do not see themselves accurately, they tend to gravitate towards negative behavior or negative people.

Our response was to create a collection of affirmations and daily activities that can be used as a building block to enhance your child's emotional well-being. We understand how important it is to impact their emotional health early, therefore, this guide was designed to be utilized in your child's formative years. But we want to encourage you that it is never too late! We would love to hear how these exercises are impacting your child's life.

~ DAY ONE~

Affirmation: You are a gift from God and your life was a divinely orchestrated event.

Activity: Write your child a letter about how happy you were when they were born. It is important to share with your child how their birth impacted your life and the life of your family.

~ DAY TWO ~

Affirmation: You are fearfully and wonderfully made. You are strong, courageous and fearless. Fear has no place in your life today!

Activity: Have your child write down the top three things that make them afraid. Use this information to initiate a discussion as well as develop tools that can counteract those feelings, e.g. If your child is afraid of water schedule some swimming lessons.

I am afraid of:

1. _____
2. _____
3. _____

~ DAY THREE~

Affirmation: You are loving, compassionate and generous. You think of others before you think of yourself.

Activity: Have your child pledge to send a donation to a charitable organization monthly. Hold them accountable for fulfilling their obligation every month by committing to a specific day and putting it as a reminder on your calendar. To find a charity we recommend *www.charitynavigator.com*.

~ DAY FOUR ~

Affirmation: You are responsible and will make significant contributions to our society. You are an answer to a problem and will make a significant impact on your generation.

Activity: Develop five small assignments to help your child be responsible and add value to their home, school, church, sports team, or organization, etc....

My Assignments:

1. _____

2. _____

3. _____

4. _____

5. _____

~ DAY FIVE~

Affirmation: You are greatly loved and accepted for the wonderful person that you are.

Activity: Give your child 10 hug coupons redeemable at any time! (*Hug coupons are in the back of the book.*)

~ DAY SIX~

Affirmation: You are full of purpose, ingenuity, and creativity.

Activity: Start a vision board with your child and help him/her complete it. You can visit *http://christinekane.com/offer/* and download a free guide.

~ DAY SEVEN~

Affirmation: Today, you are friendly and helpful.

Activity: Help your child plan a play date with four of his/her closest friends. In addition, encourage your child to play with someone who looks like they need a friend.

Planning your play date:

Your friends:

1._____

2._____

3._____

4._____

Play date ideas:

1._____

2._____

3._____

4._____

Date of event: _____

~ DAY EIGHT~

Affirmation: Today, you are focused, determined and hard working.

Activity: Read a biography with your child of one person who you feel will have a significant impact on them. Continue with this activity until the book is complete. Or if time is a factor Wikipedia is a great source of information.

GEARED FOR GREATNESS

~ DAY NINE~

Affirmation: Today, there is nothing you cannot accomplish and the word "can't" is not in your vocabulary.

Activity: Spend 30 minutes over ice cream (all the trimmings!) letting your child share their goals and aspirations.

Things I want to accomplish

1._____

2._____

3._____

4._____

5._____

6._____

7._____

8._____

9._____

10._____

~ DAY TEN~

Affirmation: Today, you make good choices to keep your body healthy.

Activity: Spend 30 minutes exercising with your child and discuss making healthy food choices. Once a week choose a healthy meal to prepare for your entire family.

~ DAY ELEVEN~

Affirmation: Today, you are forgiving and are making amends with everyone who has hurt you or made you mad.

Activity: Apologize to your child for anything you have done or said that may have been hurtful. Encourage him/her to ask for forgiveness from anyone they may have hurt.

~ DAY TWELVE~

Affirmation: Today, you know how to ask for help when things get too difficult for you.

Activity: Start praying with your child for five minutes a day. Teaching them they can always get help from God.

~ DAY THIRTEEN

Affirmations: Today, you love and respect your parent(s), your brother(s) and your sister(s).

Activity: Take a family photo and place it on the refrigerator as a constant reminder that your child has a wonderful family. Reinforce in your child the importance of respecting each member of the family.

~ DAY FOURTEEN~

Affirmations: Today, I am developing productive life habits.

Activity: Help your child identify and write down three things they would like to change about their behavior. Develop a 30-day plan to change them. Have your child come back to you at the end of 30-days to report their progress.

Things I want to Change:

1._____

2._____

3._____

~ DAY FIFTEEN~

Affirmation: Today, you have a grateful heart.

Activity: Write down at least three things that you and your child are thankful for about each other. Then swap notes and use this as a constant source of encouragement.

~ DAY SIXTEEN~

Affirmation: Today, you have an excellent attitude.

Activity: Have your child help you prepare dinner for the family.

~ DAY SEVENTEEN~

Affirmation: Today, you love yourself unconditionally and are happy with your surroundings.

Activity: Have your child make a self-esteem collage about the things they love about himself/herself. Frame it and hang it in his/her room.

~ DAY EIGHTEEN~

Affirmation: Today, you are an excellent student and you have a great memory.

Activity: Play a board game with your child that enhances academic aptitude.

Games we suggest:

- Monopoly
- Scrabble
- Boggle
- Jenga
- Pictionary

~ DAY NINETEEN~

Affirmation: Today, you are neat and organized.

Activity: Teach your child how to do their chores the way you want them done. Encourage them to do an excellent job and reward them for it. In addition, help them organize their room.

~ DAY TWENTY~

Affirmation: Today, you are Geared for Greatness!

Activity: Read three of your favorite chapters in *Geared for Greatness* to your child and discuss the meaning and importance of each topic.

~ DAY TWENTY-ONE~

Affirmation: Today, you deserve all that is good and you are letting go of negative emotions.

Activity: Take a simple walk around the corner with your child enjoying the beauty of nature. Breathe in and out deeply receiving the peace of God.

GEARED FOR GREATNESS

~ DAY TWENTY-TWO ~

Affirmation: Today, your mind is filled only with loving, healthy, positive and prosperous thoughts.

Activity: Spend 30 minutes with your child thinking and talking about good things. Reinforce positive communication for the next seven days.

~ DAY TWENTY-THREE ~

Affirmation: Today, you are not concerned about what other people think or say about you. You are being the best person you know how to be.

Activity: Give your child a special gift!

~ DAY TWENTY-FOUR ~

Affirmation: Today, everything is working out for you and you are achieving all your goals.

Activity: Help your child establish two short-term and two long-term age appropriate goals. As the parent, follow through is extremely important. It teaches your child that you care and that you keep your word.

Your goals:

Short term: (two weeks – three weeks)

1._____

2._____

Long term: (30 days – 6 months)

1._____

2._____

~ DAY TWENTY- FIVE ~

Affirmation: Today, you will not worry and you are allowing your heart to be filled with peace.

Activity: Plan a pillow fight and family slumber party! Joy is a powerful force, which enables a person to cope with the difficulties of life. There is nothing more joyous than spending time with your family.

~ DAY TWENTY- SIX ~

Affirmation: Today, I am an avid learner, and I am interested in those things that have social and moral value.

Activity: Limit the number of minutes that your child engages in social media, the internet or video games. Assist your child in learning something new. I would recommend *www.onthisday.com*, which is a powerful source of information about events that happened the day they were born.

~ DAY TWENTY- SEVEN ~

Affirmation: Today, you embrace the fact that everyone is special and you will be kind to those around you.

Activity: Develop a "you're special" award. Celebrate one member of the family once a month. Decorate his/her bedroom, give them a card, or serve them breakfast in bed. In addition to that, have your child pick one person at school who they can give the award to, i.e. best friend, teacher, principle, etc.…

~ DAY TWENTY- EIGHT ~

Affirmation: Today, you will only listen to and watch things that bring you happiness and joy!

Activity: Have your family turn off their phones and television for one night and play a game, listen to music or just talk and enjoy each other's company.

~ DAY TWENTY- NINE ~

Affirmation: Today, you do everything with an excellent spirit. You will not cut corners or take shortcuts.

Activity: Have your child help you with a task that you have been putting off for a long time. Also, encourage your child to clean up after themselves for the week. Be diligent to turn the week into a lifelong habit.

~ DAY THIRTY ~

Affirmation: Today, you take responsibility for keeping this world beautiful.

Activity: Plant a garden and pick up trash around the neighborhood.

Final Thoughts

In closing I'd like to share that on February 16, 2006, I donated a kidney to a fellow member of my church. This by far, apart from raising my children, has been up to now, the most significant accomplishment in my life. As I shared in the book, I am determined to leave this world completely empty of everything that God has deposited in me. A dear friend of mine once said, *"Never rob the world of the gifts that God has given you. If you are going to rob anything, rob the grave and leave this world spent of all."*

    Although I do not know your religious beliefs, I want to take the opportunity to share mine. I am a Christian and have been one for the last 32 years. I feel that it is my spiritual responsibility to at least give you the opportunity to accept Christ. Christ in my life has made all the difference in who I am.

    Being a Christian has not shielded me from life's changes or challenges. I, like everyone else, have had my share of tragedies, mistakes, and mishaps. To share a few, I lost my mother to cancer when I was 19 years old and in my first year of college. I lost a child six months into my pregnancy. I am a survivor of molestation and domestic abuse. I have suffered the shame of divorce and my father abandoned all five of his children; I did not meet him in person until he came to my mother's funeral. Yet, my being in Christ and Christ being in me has given me peace and inner strength to be an overcomer.

    God's heart is open to receive you and it does not matter where you have been or what you have done. The grace of God is sufficient for all who come to Him. If you are already a believer, you know the blessing of this truth.

    The Bible says we can approach God's throne of grace with confidence (Hebrews 4:16). It is my prayer that you at least give Christ the opportunity to show you how much He loves and cares for you.

If you feel so inclined below is a prayer of salvation:

Dear Lord, I admit that I am a sinner. I have done many things that do not please you. I have lived my life for myself and I am sorry. I repent and turn away from a life of sin and ask you to forgive me. I believe that you died on the cross to save me, and Jesus rose from the dead to empower me to live this new life. I believe you did what I could not do for myself and for that I am grateful. I come to you now and ask you to take control of my life. I give it to you. I surrender. As I embark on this new journey, help me to live every day in a way that pleases you. I love you Lord, and I thank you for the peace that comes in knowing I will spend all of eternity with you (Romans 10-9-10).

HUG COUPON

REEDEMABLE AT ANYTIME

HUG COUPON

REEDEMABLE AT ANYTIME

HUG COUPON

REEDEMABLE AT ANYTIME

HUG COUPON

REEDEMABLE AT ANYTIME

www.ingramcontent.com/pod-product-compliance
Lightning Source LLC
LaVergne TN
LVHW051048080426
835508LV00019B/1772